LIBERTY'S PROVENANCE

The launch of the first of 2,710 Liberty ships, the SS *Patrick Henry*, on 27 September 1941.
But, where did the design originate? This book explores the full history.

LIBERTY'S PROVENANCE

The Evolution of the Liberty Ship from its Sunderland Origins

John Henshaw

Seaforth
PUBLISHING

DEDICATION

To Robert Cyril Thompson, CBE, 1907–1967
The unsung hero in the evolution of the Liberty ship

First published in Great Britain in 2019 by
Seaforth Publishing,
A division of Pen & Sword Books Ltd,
47 Church Street,
Barnsley S70 2AS

www.seaforthpublishing.com

British Library Cataloguing in Publication Data
A catalogue record for this book is available from the British Library
ISBN 978 1 5267 5063 1(hardback)
ISBN 978 1 5267 5065 5 (kindle)
ISBN 978 1 5267 5064 8 (epub)

Pen & Sword Books Limited incorporates the imprints of Atlas, Archaeology, Aviation, Discovery, Family History, Fiction, History, Maritime, Military, Military Classics, Politics, Select, Transport, True Crime, Air World, Frontline Publishing, Leo Cooper, Remember When, Seaforth Publishing, The Praetorian Press, Wharncliffe Local History, Wharncliffe Transport, Wharncliffe True Crime and White Owl.

Typeset and designed by Neil Sayer
Printed and bound in India by Replika Press Pvt Ltd

CONTENTS

ACKNOWLEDGEMENTS AND NOTES ON THE DRAWINGS

Ithank Angela DeRoy-Jones who was a most helpful correspondent after I made contact with her through her website devoted to the 'Forts', 'Parks' and 'Victory' ships – fortships.tripod.com – and I would urge anyone wanting specific information as to individual Canadian-built ships to visit that site. She was also kind enough to provide me with a fold-out drawing that was missing from my copy of Heal's book.

As with my previous book, *Town Class Destroyers: A Critical Assessment*, my son Andrew – a professional photographer – was of considerable assistance in helping to select and then improve the limited number of photographs to choose from and I thank him for another labour of love in this regard. If some of the photographs are of poor quality, it is because they were the best of what was available but considered essential to the narrative.

I am indebted to the Naval History and Heritage Command whose collection of photographs is invaluable. While not always of the best quality due to their age, unlike so many sourced from the Internet, their provenance is unquestionable and this quality alone sets them apart.

The Tyne & Wear Archives & Museums were most helpful in going beyond normal customer service in photographing the original General Arrangement drawing of *Empire Liberty* which was too large to fit their copier and I thank them for this generosity. Miss Lizzie Baker, the Archives Lead, was particularly helpful and patient with my many requests.

The searlecanada.org site was one I discovered like so many quite by accident and I kept coming back to it to either look for or check information. Thank you, Peter F Searle.

At various times I found links to very poor-quality copies of individual pages of Lloyd's Register of Shipping – often through wrecksite.eu – that gave valuable information simply unobtainable elsewhere or obtainable but unsubstantiated or simply wrong in other sources.

The drawings in this book which form an integral part of the story of how the Liberty ship came into being have all been prepared by me using AutoCAD. With CAD you draw in 1:1 scale. That is, you draw the actual dimensions – or what you reckon to be the actual dimensions. If you had a printer and paper big enough, you could reproduce the plans full size. So, what you see on the computer monitor at any time is a bit like looking through a big telescope from the wrong end. What you see is smaller . . . much, much smaller than the real thing.

While I work solely in the metric system, I have chosen to write the book using measurements in the Imperial system as this was the system of the time. There did not seem any point, for instance, in using solely the metric system and stating that, for example, the United States Maritime Commission (USMC) C1 class ships were those under 121.921m in length, that the C2 class were to be those no longer than 137.617m in length. Had the metric system been used by America then – and it still isn't! – the USMC may well have chosen 120m and 140m respectively as nice round numbers.

My starting point – indeed, from memory the thing which stimulated the process that became this book – was discovering sixteen drawings of the Liberty Ship ss *Arthur M Huddell* that had been redrawn as a recording project co-sponsored by the Historic American Engineering Record (HAER) and the US Maritime Administration (MARAD), Department of Transportation and also by finding drawings of three versions of Liberty ships on the Historic Naval Ship Association's website general plans online. These, collectively, gave me the sort of details previously missing as to the frame spacings of the hull that allowed me to do a simple framing grid. The first twelve frames, from the bow moving aft, are at 24in spacings, the next twenty-seven are at 27in spacings and thereafter at 30in spacing until Frame 162 when they revert to 24in (609.6mm) spacings. One of the best source drawings of

***

the Liberty ship shows what looks to be a 7in expansion joint at critical Frame 88 – the aft bulkhead of Hold No 3 which is also the forward bulkhead of the boiler room. It may be two frames, 7in apart. (Note: British shipyards number frames from the rudder post forward and US shipyards number frames from some nominal point in the bow aft.)

Why was the frame spacing important? Ships are constructed on a modular basis – the frame spacings dictate where bulkheads and where other structural elements are located. Because I have to create my drawings by scaling off other drawings that when printed may only fit on, say, A3-sized paper, when I work out a dimension and transfer it to the CAD drawing, its relationship to the framing grid determines the final location. For instance, deckhouses and masts will line up with a frame because they will be supported on the beam that spans the frame or will be a continuation of the bulkhead beneath. Deck openings fit between deck beams. Scuppers, ventilators and portholes always fit between frames. Also, you get to be able to 'read' the mind of the original designers who worked in feet and inches. When it came to a radiused corner, they didn't use some odd number; they liked 4in, 6in, 8in, or 12in or 24in. Very often I'd scale off a drawing to find the answer was those nice round number favoured by draftsmen: 6ft, 8ft, 10ft etc, or especially those divisible, in this instance, by 30in because of the frame spacing.

The drawings are reproduced at 1:600 scale. I should state at this point that the purpose of the drawings is not to provide a definitive set of drawings, or a reference work for modelmakers. The drawings are a means of making comparisons between one ship and another, to see the progression of the design from its beginnings and to identify what basic changes occurred. As such the amount of detail on the drawings is by no means all-embracing. I would have liked, for example, to have a detailed drawing of the deck winches of each type. Instead I found one winch type and used it for all. At 1:600 scale, a lot of that detail is lost anyway as, no matter how good a printer may be and using the finest line possible, it is simply not possible to distinguish all the detail so the purists will, undoubtedly, find fault. If I had the original drawings I would have used them. In some instances, indeed in many instances, because the drawings I have had to work from have been basic to say the least, I have had to guess – calculated guesses based on photographs if available – what sort of detail to include to give an overall impression rather than a definitive drawing. A good example of this is the drawing of the Z-EC2-S-C5 Boxed Aircraft Transport version of the Liberty ship. I was unable to uncover any drawing at all so had to guess just how the winches might have been located to service the kingpost derricks. In the end, I don't think it's particularly relevant. What's relevant is that the drawing shows how versatile the basic design was – how it could be adapted to serve yet another role.

I trust readers will regard my particular drawings as descriptive rather than prescriptive – as a means of making comparisons between types rather than thinking of any one of them as being an absolutely factual representation. If I was ever fortunate to come across the builders' drawings it would give me great pleasure to make good all inaccuracies in a later edition.

INTRODUCTION

When it comes to the Second World War, many people will immediately bring to mind the ubiquitous Liberty ship. Like so many other instruments of war – the Spitfire fighter, the Sherman tank, the Willys Jeep, the Garand rifle, to mention just a few – the Liberty ship had its own aura, its own almost mythological persona. The very name, 'Liberty ship', in itself was catchy and emotive at a time when spirits needed the sort of uplift offered so effectively not just by those simple words but by the prodigious deeds these ships performed.

Without doubt, the Liberty ships played a hugely important role in the logistics of warfare, both in the Atlantic and the Pacific. Frederick Lane set a particular mould in his 1951 book, *Ships for Victory: A History of Shipbuilding Under the US Maritime Commission in World War II*, which used a painting of a Liberty ship on the cover to link, principally, the Liberty ship with victory. Peter Elphick took this further and called his 2001 book, *Liberty: The Ships that Won the War*. The title says, in effect, they made the difference between winning and losing. It says: no Liberty ships, therefore defeat. I think that's an overreach – many steps too far. No single type of ship, as such, won the Second World War or, indeed, secured a victory. The Liberty ships did, undoubtedly, make a difference – just like the *Fletcher*-class destroyers or *Essex*-class aircraft carriers of the United States Navy, or the 'Flower'-class corvettes of the Royal Navy. On the other hand, Gus Bourneuf Jr's book published in 1990 made the more modest and reasonable claim in its title: *Workhorse of the Fleet: A History of the Liberty Ships*. Most Liberty ships served outside what we could think of as 'The Fleet' – that is a naval fleet or, more particularly, the United States Navy's fleet and served under very imaginable merchant marine flag well beyond their designed life expectancy, thereby defying their critics. They were converted to other uses, extended in length, re-engined and were indeed the workhorses of the much-depleted post-war merchant fleet – something they were never expected to do.

The much-maligned Liberty ship – the 'ugly duckling' of *The Times*, the 'dreadful-looking object' in President Roosevelt's opinion – proved to be an extraordinarily versatile and adaptable ship. Instead of performing in only one-way, did-its-job voyages, it was adopted by the USN for a wide variety of tasks both during the Second World War and for many years thereafter, finally serving a role in the Cold War that was never imagined in 1940.

But there have been too many myths, too much hyperbole, too many falsehoods perpetuated over time as to how the Liberty ship came into being. While they were all built in the United States – all 2,710 of them (and this number is generally accepted but quite often debated) and this was a truly remarkable achievement – they were not, as most people have been led to believe, a totally American-conceived and developed product.

So, just exactly what was the Liberty ship's provenance? Their origins, the very essence of their being, the drawings and specifications that they grew from came from a small shipyard in Sunderland, on the banks of the River Wear in the Municipal Borough of County Durham in Britain, well before America entered the Second World War in December 1941. This book sets the record straight, once and for all, as to how this came about.

But first, the requirement for the Liberty ship – why it was needed in the first place – has to be seen in context.

German U-boat campaigns in both World Wars led to a need for emergency merchant shipbuilding and parallels can be drawn as to how Britain and the United States of America responded to the challenges.

Both wars saw a Battle of the Atlantic – their similarities greater than their dissimilarities. Clearly the First World War's battle was fought in a smaller operational area, with significantly smaller and less technically capable forces. Unlike in the Second World War, the Germans pursued an interrupted unrestricted submarine warfare policy as it feared drawing the United States into the conflict. In all other respects, the aims and objectives were the same – to sever Britain's lines of communication and trade with its Empire and with the industrial powerhouse of the United States. In both conflicts it almost succeeded.

Both battles were a simple matter of arithmetic. To win them, the British needed to be able to replace shipping at least at the same rate and preferably at a greater rate at which it was being sunk and to sink submarines faster than they could be replaced. Professor A J Marder in his five-volume work, *From the Dreadnought to Scapa Flow*, goes even further. He suggests that sinking submarines was a bonus. What mattered was that ships delivered their cargoes regularly and adequately, and that it did not matter how many submarines the Germans had providing they were forced to keep out of the way and the ships got through.[1] It's an interesting concept because it assumes that the advantages of one override the disadvantages of the other, that the volume of the logistics delivered, the materiel to sustain war and the people who wage it, would eventually be the determining factor, not the enemy's submarine losses.

The fact remains that both wars saw an incredible amount of tonnage lost, primarily in the Atlantic but also in the Mediterranean: almost 13 million tons in the First World War and over 27.5 million tons in the Second. This tonnage was replaced – not all as and when it was required, but eventually.

This book describes how this was done – how a transatlantic bridge of ships was built – from a design that had its beginnings in 1935 in a then out-of-work British shipyard.

John Henshaw
Cape Schanck,
Australia,
(January 2019)

CHAPTER 1: THE BATTLE OF THE ATLANTIC, 1914–1918

Historians are divided as to whether it is correct to refer to the German submarine warfare conducted principally against Britain between 4 August 1914 and 6 April 1917 and against Britain and the United States of America between 6 April 1917 and 11 November 1918 as being the First Battle of the Atlantic. The main reason given why not is that, unlike the 1939–45 conflict, it did not involve the Atlantic as a whole – that is, the North Atlantic (including the Arctic) and the South Atlantic – but only the Western Approaches to the British Isles, the North Sea and the English Channel/Strait of Dover.

However, for the purposes of this book, I choose to side with those historians who describe that 1914–18 U-boat threat to Britain's transatlantic supply lines as the First Battle of the Atlantic. I do so because its purpose was identical to that of 1939–45 – that is, to cut those very supply lines, to sever those traditional trade routes that made and sustained Britain's empire, to reduce Britain's ability to wage war and to feed its people. For example, at the time, Britain imported 100 per cent of its sugar, cocoa and chocolate; 79 per cent of its grain; 64.5 per cent of its butter; and 40 per cent of its meat. Nearly two-thirds of the

The British cargo ship SS *Maplewood* under attack by the German submarine *U-35* on 7 April 1917. (www.theatlantic.com)

calorific intake of the British people came from abroad. Supplies of industrial materials such as cotton, oil or rubber were completely dependent on imports. Imports provided a large share of the ore or metals worked by British factories. Three-quarters of the wool woven in British mills was shipped in from overseas.[1]

That commonality with 1939–45 cannot be denied. The fact that it took place over a smaller sphere of operations was a factor of the available technology at the time insofar as submarines were concerned and, unlike in 1940, the Germans did not gain access to French west-coast ports for easier access to the Atlantic thereby effectively increasing the range of their submarines.

Terraine quotes the words of an anonymous officer:

Being an island was now a liability, lay the grim facts of geography. No ruses, no stratagems, could alter the inescapable truth that all shipping seeking to enter British ports must ultimately follow certain obvious and unchangeable routes.[2]

Fayle says there were 'three great cones of approach':[3]

- From the Mediterranean and South Atlantic to Bristol and the Channel ports.
- From the Caribbean and South American ports to Bristol and Liverpool (via the south of Ireland).
- From the northern American ports and Canada to Liverpool and the Clyde (via the north of Ireland).

Lord Jellicoe added a fourth:

- A north-about route to the East Coast ports via the Orkneys.

These 'cones' made it easy for the U-boats to sit and wait for the steady stream of ships, going to and fro.

According to Terraine 12.85 million tons of merchant shipping was lost in the First World War.[4] Some two-thirds of this was lost in the Western Approaches.[5] Also, 153 of the 178 U-boats sunk (86 per cent) during the war, if not all sunk there, were assigned to those forces operating in the Western Approaches. These are further reasons for giving credence to the term, First Battle of the Atlantic.

The Battle can be broken down into the following phases:

6 AUGUST 1914 — END 1914

This was essentially an anti-Royal Navy campaign in the North Sea with limited successes. The most significant effect, however, was that the Grand Fleet dispersed from its previously thought safe Scapa Flow anchorage strategically placed in the Orkney Islands. Germany only had twenty-eight U-boats in its whole fleet at the time, of which all but seven were in the North Sea. However, at any time, less than half-a-dozen would be on patrol.

Merchant shipping tonnage sunk 1914:
British 241,201, Other 71,471 tons, TOTAL 312,672 tons.[6]

1915

The Royal Navy established an effective blockade of the North Sea and in February 1915 Germany retaliated with a policy of Unrestricted Submarine Warfare instituted against all British shipping in a declared 'War Zone'. Whereas in the past a set of 'Cruiser Rules' had generally applied – that is, submarines would stop a merchant ship and search it, and, if carrying contraband cargo and bound for a British port or for a British-controlled port, allow the crew to take to the boats and then sink the ship with demolition charges or gunfire – this was abandoned in favour of what was basically a 'shoot-first-and-ask-no-questions-later' policy. In reality, it was impractical for a submarine to surface, stop a vessel, transfer a crew to inspect the vessel and find sufficient members to form a prize crew from amongst its own small crew to convey it to a suitable port. Neutral ships were not exempt although they were not specifically targeted. A system of

safe-conduct passes was introduced by the Germans late in the war for ships that guaranteed not to call at enemy harbours. Quite how such guarantees were policed is unknown. The sinking of the Cunard liner *Lusitania* on 7 May 1915 with the loss of 1,198 lives brought worldwide opprobrium – particularly from the neutral USA because of the 128 of its citizens lost in the sinking – but did not dissuade Germany from continuing or even reducing the unrestricted submarine warfare campaign. But, what should be understood, that this was from a flotilla that numbered between only three and four U-boats at sea at any given time.

Merchant shipping tonnage sunk 1915:
British 855,731 tons, Other 452,265 tons, TOTAL 1,307,996 tons.

1916

There was a temporary diversion of some U-boat activity to minelaying and also in order to try and effect ambushes on elements of the Grand Fleet. The basic principle was that the German fleet would turn away and try and lure the Grand Fleet into a waiting line of U-boats. The tactic met without success, the Grand Fleet preferring to pursue on the flanks, expecting an ambush on the line of advance. Protests from the United States caused a temporary reversion to 'board and search' policies in April. However, the policy of Unrestricted Submarine Warfare was debated in August – the major issue being the threat of

A First World War Atlantic convoy. Second World War convoys had more columns but with fewer ships in them.

dragging the United States into the War. Despite the debate, the effect was that September and October tonnages rose and the 'sinking without warning' for 1916 rose 29 per cent.[7]

Merchant shipping tonnage sunk 1916:
British 1,237,634 tons, Other 1,089,692 tons, TOTAL 2,327,326 tons.

1917

On 1 February, Germany announced a significant increase in the area of the 'War Zone'. This year saw an increase in the number of U-boats (111 in February – forty-nine were in the North Sea flotilla, thirty-three in the Flanders flotilla) and a concerted effort to starve Britain into submission. However, this blockade, despite the alarming numbers below, was not as effective as the Royal Navy's surface blockade of Germany.

The system of convoying merchant ships rather than proceeding independently was instituted in May and this began to cut losses. For example, in April some 880,000 tons had been lost (Terraine) and losses decline markedly from this point. Why it took so long to institute the system is difficult to understand. Convoys go back to Roman times. They were used to defend the annual wool and wine trade between England and its possessions in Aquitaine, by the Spanish to protect their flotta from Elizabethan privateers, by the Dutch to and from the Netherlands and, of course, in the Napoleonic Wars. My own homeland, Australia, was settled by the First Fleet of eleven ships sailing more than 15,000 miles in convoy over three months. Winston Churchill summed up the advantages of convoy in wartime in his book, *The World Crisis*, of 1923:

> The size of the sea is so vast that the difference between the size of a convoy and the size of a single ship in comparison shrinks almost to insignificance. There was in fact very nearly as good a chance of a convoy of forty ships in close order slipping unperceived between the patrolling U-boats as there was for a single ship, and each time this happened forty ships escaped instead of

one . . . The concentration of ships greatly reduced the numbers of targets in a given area and thus made it more difficult for the submarines to locate their prey.

After the USA entered the conflict, the number of ships crossing the Atlantic increased yet the proportion of losses fell. Conversely, U-boat losses increased as anti-submarine techniques improved and minefields were extended.

Merchant shipping tonnage sunk 1917:
British 3,729,785 tons, Other 2,506,093 tons, TOTAL 6,235,878 tons.

1918

On 21 October, all U-boats were recalled. Terraine states that the campaign lasted just under twenty-one months.[8] This does not take into account the first 'bout'. The number of sinkings, tonnages lost in this period speak for themselves, reflecting both the efficiency of the convoy system, the anti-submarine activities, lessons learnt and the very large increase in the number of ships being convoyed. By the end of the war nearly 17,000 ships had sailed under escort across the Atlantic with only 1 per cent sunk.

Merchant shipping tonnage sunk 1918:
British 1,694,749 tons, Other 972,193 tons, TOTAL 2,666,942 tons.[9]

***

Of the 12,037,548 tons of shipping lost during the First World War, Britain and its Dominions lost 7,923,023 tons according to the Federal Reserve Bulletin of February 1921 or 7,759,090 tons according to Terraine. The former represents 65.8 per cent of the total while the latter represents 60.6 per cent of the 12,850,814 tons total provided by Terraine. The former specifically excludes non-war losses while the latter does include British and foreign fishing vessels and steam and sailing vessels of all sizes. and whichever total is accepted, this shipping had to be replaced, and partly was.

CHAPTER 2: BRITAIN'S EMERGENCY SHIPS OF THE FIRST WORLD WAR

The British were slow off the mark in establishing convoys as a means of reducing the shipping losses. They were equally as slow in coming to grips with a viable solution to replacing the lost shipping. The loss of skilled workers to the various armed forces came at a time when the demand for their skills was greater than ever. Purchasing ships overseas – in what was basically a seller's market – provided only a small fraction of what was necessary to keep the situation stable, let alone reverse it, and severely reduced gold reserves.

Finally, at the very end of 1916, a Shipping Controller was appointed and a Merchant Shipbuilding Advisory Committee established. The logical decision was reached to embark on a programme to build ships of the minimum number of standard designs that would be simple and quick to build yet still yield the maximum amount of cargo space for the minimum expenditure of cost in labour and materials. To complicate the issue, the Royal Navy stuck its proverbial oar in and required

that the traditional forecastle be abandoned as crew accommodation as they felt it was potentially most unsafe in the event of torpedoing. Further, it was required that low silhouettes be achieved via collapsible masts and derricks and that funnels – normally tall to ensure a good draft and to keep smoke clear of the bridge (particularly in following winds) – be kept as short as possible. These were items that worked both against cost and time.

The idea of reproducing a proven design over and over again is the very essence of mass production – the difference between the Industrial Revolution and the cottage industry that preceded it. Shipbuilding, other than warships, tended not to follow this path with individual shipbuilders following their own, preferred practices – often limited to the size of the slipways available to them. Attempts at standardisation had been made – the unconventional 'whaleback', Doxford's turret ship, the trunk-deck ship, Isherwood's longitudinal-framed and arc-form ship

An F Type, apparently the uninspiringly named *War Bothwell*. Her counter stern marks her as a Thompson-built ship. Doxford-built ships had a pronounced rounded cruiser stern as shown in the drawing on p 15. (shipsnostalgia.com)

(with rounded sides) and, later, Doxford's diesel-engined 'Economy Tramp'. Some of these were not so much driven by economising on building but rather as tax-cheating devices due to interpretations of regulations such as canal charges.

The first emergency ship design was a pair from Harland & Wolff of Belfast and were called the A and B Class Standard Tramp. The A was a single deck and the B a double deck with greater capacity. Both were 412ft 0in LOA x 52ft 0in beam x 25ft 0in draft with a displacement of 11,375 tons and had coal-fired Vertical Triple Expansion (VTE) engines operating a single screw driving the ships at 11 knots. There may have been fifty-four A Types built and 143 B Types built. It is difficult to be precise. Some ships were allocated numbers but not given names, other were allocated names but not numbers, others were given both

and orders were cancelled. The only photographs I could find were from the Imperial War Museum (IWM) collection of the first of these ships launched was SS *War Shamrock* in August 1917 – only fifteen months, at best, before the Armistice. The photographs depict a very conventional, centre-island ship with counter stern but, somewhat unusually, closely-spaced kingposts in place of a single, centreline mast serving fore and aft hatches. Harland & Wolff achieved some remarkable building times – twenty-four weeks from keel-laying to completion.

The next series were scaled-down versions of the A and B Types suitable for smaller shipyards – the C Type being a at 331ft 0in LBP and 5,050 DWT and the D Type at 285ft 0in LBP and 2,980 DWT. There was a two-decker E Type version also. In order to reduce waste, the propulsion units were standardised: A,

A AND B TYPE STANDARD SHIP

These were the most numerous of the cargo ships. The folding kingposts are shown as broken lines.

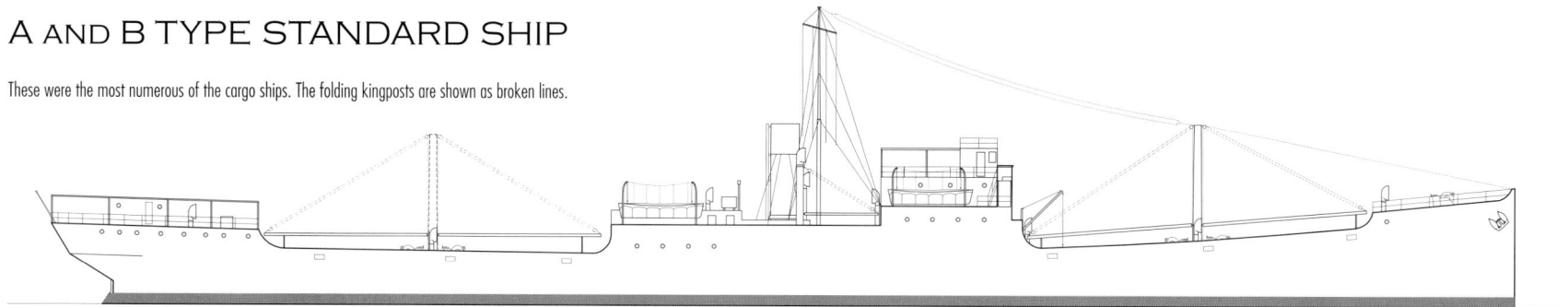

C TYPE STANDARD SHIP

The C Type was a scaled-down version of the A and B Type.

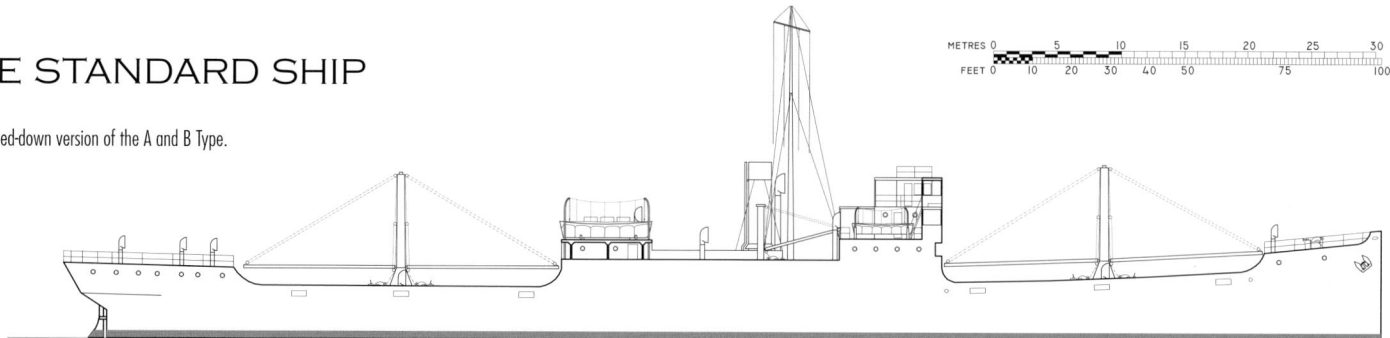

F TYPE STANDARD SHIP

The bulbous cruiser stern marks the ship as built by Wm Doxford & Sons Ltd, Sunderland.

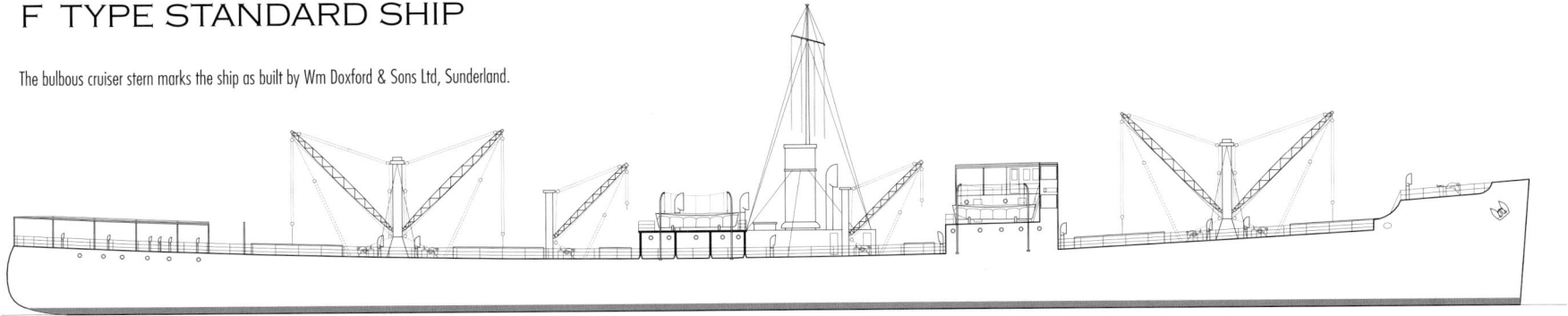

F1 TYPE STANDARD SHIP

Designed and built by Joseph L Thompson & Sons Ltds, Sunderland. Note the counter stern.

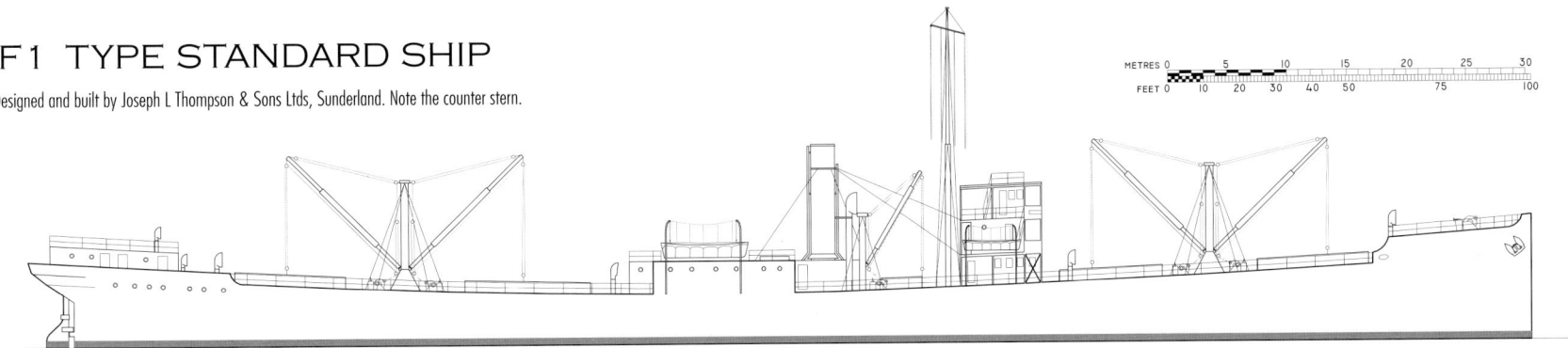

METRES	0	5	10	15	20	25	30
FEET	0	10 20 30	40 50		75		100

B and E Types having 2,500 VTE and C and D Types with a smaller VTE – the C having water-tube boilers.

The F and F1 Types were large ships, being 441ft 6in LBP x 55ft 6in beam x 28ft 7½in draft and being 6,440 GRT, 10,795 DWT and a displacement of 14,495 tons, and 400ft 0in LBP x 53ft 0in beam x 26ft 4ft draft and being 5,680 GRT, 9,000 DWT and 11,935 tons displacement. Both were capable of 12 knots from their VTE and single screw. These were shelter deck type fitted with 'tween decks. Twenty-four were built. Joseph L

Thompson & Sons of Sunderland were the Parent Builders of the F Type[1] and apparently the designers.[2] We will hear much more of this shipbuilding company later. Northumberland Shipbuilding Company of Howdon-on-Tyne were the Parent Builders for the F1 Type.

The G Type were a class of twenty-two fast – 13 knots – refrigerated ships. Fourteen were twin-screw with VTE power and the remainder were single-screw with double-reduction geared turbines. They were 465ft 0in LOA, 450ft 0in LBP x 58ft

N TYPE PREFABRICATED SHIP

There is no mistaking the austere and ungainly lines of Harland & Wolff's N or National-class prefabricated ships.

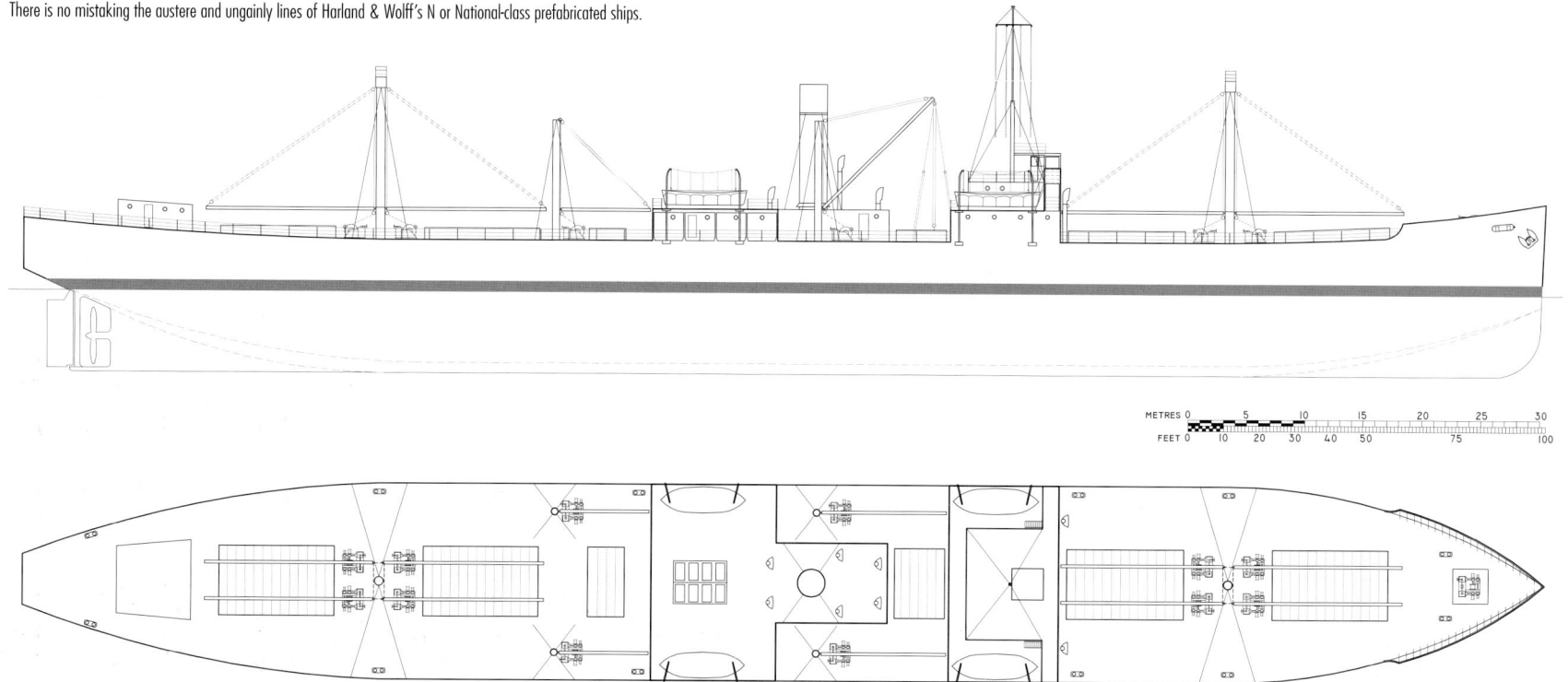

| METRES 0 | 5 | 10 | 15 | 20 | 25 | 30 |
| FEET 0 | 10 | 20 | 30 | 40 | 50 | 75 | 100 |

0in beam x 29ft 0in draft and being 8,000 GRT, 10,800 DWT and a displacement of 16,000 tons. There was also a small H Type and various coasters.

Certainly, the most important in realistically addressing the problem of quick and cheap production, was the National or N class which was as unconventional as the A and B class were conventional. Here, the naval architect's design philosophy and the shipbuilder's usual methods were thrown out the window and a completely new and fresh approach was applied to the problem. In order to simplify, cheapen and speed up construction, there was no sheer to the deck – save a small upturn at bow and stern

– there was no camber to the decks and for ease of construction the hull shape was basically a box in section. There was no keel as such, the hull being entirely flat-bottomed, and instead of a conventional round turn to the bilges the bilge was a simple 45° chamfer ending at the stern in a triangular transom. All of these 'features' facilitated some degree of prefabrication – the first in the history of steel shipbuilding. These were ugly but functional ships that were prefabricated by bridge builders and engineering works not normally associated with shipbuilding.

Again, this was a Harland & Wolff design and dated from 1917. The design originally called for turbine propulsion and

A well-camouflaged N Type ship, *War Climax*. (Tyne & Wear Archives & Museums)

water-tube boilers – a contradiction if ever there was one. Why build a simple, no-frills hull and then put expensive, sophisticated propulsion in it? That doesn't make a lot of sense. But, the rationale was, apparently, that it was easier to transport these more compact items from the places of manufacture to the shipyards. Sixteen of the thirty-four – again I am not absolutely sure of the numbers – were so equipped, the others having VTE and Scotch boilers made on or near site. These ships were 428ft 0in LOA, 411ft 6in LBP x 55ft 5½in beam x 28ft 0in draft and being 6,590 GRT, 10,500 DWT and a displacement of 14,190 tons.

Unfortunately, most of the emergency ships were completed after the war was over – in a lot of cases well after – and records as to exactly what ships saw service are difficult to determine. Completion dates can be a guide but they don't necessarily mean that a ship went into useful service at that time. Trials had to be conducted, defects remedied, crews found and made familiar with the new ship, passage to an embarkation port, taking on ballast and/or some sort of cargo, forming into a westbound convoy and so forth all took time. For most of the information

War Music. Note the pronounced transom stern. (collections.tepapa.govt.nz)

above, Mitchell and Sawyer's book *British Standard Ships of World War I* was the only reliable source.

All emergency-built ships were given a 'War' prefix. While this provided some emotive names like *War Breaker*, *War Freedom* and *War Honour*, it also produced some equally uninspiring and insipid names like *War Beryl*, *War Pink* and *War Daisy*.

Across the Atlantic, a shipbuilding programme in United States shipyards was initiated by the British Government through Cunard's New York office and was taken over by the United States government and extended.[3]

A very similar approach was taken by the United States to the problem resulting, particularly, in two designs:

- Emergency Fleet Corporation (EFC) Design 1022 was Hog Island Standard Fabricated Type A freighter, and
- Emergency Fleet Corporation (EFC) Design 1024 was Hog Island Standard Fabricated Type B passenger ship.

Chapter 3: The United States Shipping Board and the Emergency Fleet Corporation

In June 1914 Britain and its Dominions had by far the largest fleet of merchants ship over 100 tons – 10,123 ships totalling 20,523,706 tons or 45.2 per cent of the world's 45,403,877 tons. Second place, by a huge margin, went to Germany with 2,090 ships totalling 5,134,720 tons and 11.3 per cent of the total. The United States occupied third place by tonnage but that position is confused by taking into account the Great Lakes fleet which outweighed its ocean-going fleet – 2,260,441 tons to 2,069,637 tons respectively – but represented only 579 ships as compared with 1,178 ships. Therefore, the USA's ocean-going fleet was a mere 4.6 per cent of the world's total and only slightly more than Norway (1,656 ships) and France (1,025 ships) with 4.3 per cent and 4.2 per cent of the tonnage in fourth and fifth place respectively.[1]

With a relatively small merchant fleet – compared to the size of its economy – the United States was heavily dependent on foreign shipping and British and European companies dominated the trade. This situation worsened with the outbreak of the First World War as the warring nations focused on transporting those goods most necessary to their survival to and from those ports most suitable to them rather than responding to the requirements of the American economy. In 1916 this situation became worse when in December the British Ministry of Shipping could use its powers to assign any ships to any routes that it believed were of primary importance to the nation's interests, effectively concentrating on the cross-North Atlantic route. Despite this, the British economy required the two-way flow of trade from India, Australia and New Zealand and coal exports to Argentina.

The United States Shipping Board (USSB) was created by the Merchant Marine Act of 1916 and was established in September that year 'for the purpose of encouraging, developing, and creating a naval auxiliary and naval reserve and a Merchant Marine to meet the requirements of the commerce of the United States with its territories and possessions and with foreign countries; to regulate carriers by water engaged in the foreign and interstate commerce of the United States for other purposes'.

On 16 April 1917 – just ten days after the United States entered the First World War – the USSB established the Emergency Fleet Corporation (EFC) to acquire, maintain, and operate merchant ships to meet national defence, foreign and domestic commerce. While the USSB had, it might be described, altruistic aims conceived in peacetime to restore the American Merchant Marine to its former glory, the EFC was established with one very distinct goal: build merchant ships, quickly, particularly to support the American Expeditionary Force in Europe.

The USSB changed too. It embarked on a programme of interning what were now enemy ships, entering them into the US Registry and making them ready for use. Ninety-one ships totalling almost 500,000 gross registered tons were involved. It also commandeered, or requisitioned, over 400 ships under construction in the United States – mostly for non-American clients including many British orders. Calm was restored by assurances that these requisitions would be used for war service only.

In order to undertake the new-build requirements, it was necessary to establish four new shipyards as all current yards were at capacity. Accordingly, the EFC sponsored yards at:

- Bristol, Delaware River, Pennsylvania (Merchant Shipbuilding Corporation).
- Hog Island, Delaware River, Pennsylvania (American International Shipbuilding Corporation).

Hog Island shipyard, probably taken in the early 1920s as the building berths are now vacant but showing how large the complex was to handle the original orders. (philadelpiaencyclopedia.org)

- Newark, Newark Bay, New Jersey (Submarine Boat Corporation).
- Wilmington, Cape Fear River, North Carolina (Wilmington-Carolina Shipbuilding Company).

There was no point having new yards if they were not going to be efficient. The best way to ensure efficiency, in both labour and materials, was to standardise what they were going to be building, to make that design simple, quick and easy to build. There were several designs, but one that was built in the greatest numbers – 110 – and that had the significant influence was Design 1022, more commonly referred to as the Hog Island Type A.

Chapter 4: Hog Island and Emergency Fleet Corporation Design 1022 (Type A)

In typical American 'can-do' fashion, the emergency fleet operation started with a bang rather than a whimper. A major contributor was the totally new, built-for-purpose shipyard at Hog Island on the Delaware River, at the confluence of the Schuylkill River in Pennsylvania. In 1916 this was not so much a distinct island but a dumping ground of dredging spoil – flat, uninhabited and used for grazing, apparently for pigs, hence the name. On 31 July 1917, the government let a multi-million-dollar contract on a virgin company, the American International Corporation. This company had been formed in New York on 22 November 1915, by J P Morgan interests, with major participation by Stillman's National City Bank and Rockefeller interests to engage in any kind of business, except banking and public utilities, in any country in the world. The stated purpose of the corporation was to develop domestic and foreign enterprises, to extend American activities abroad, and to promote the interests of American and foreign bankers, business and engineering (Anthony Sutton, *Wall Street and the Bolshevik Revolution*, Chapter VIII). Its subsidiary was the American International Shipbuilding Corporation – the parent to build a massive shipyard on the land another subsidiary had had the foresight to purchase some two months earlier at, apparently, a figure twenty times the land's assessed value. Dredgers immediately began to add Delaware River spoil and in December 1917 more fill was quickly added and the island was joined to the mainland. Services were extended: electricity, sewerage, railway and telephone lines. Eventually, fifty slipways, seven wet docks and a detention basin and twenty-eight outfitting docks were built along a mile and a quarter of river front. The shipyard covered 846 acres with 250 buildings. At its peak, it employed 30,000 workers (some sources credit it with as many as 35,000). From scratch, it became the largest shipyard in the world but not one in the traditional sense. Parts manufactured elsewhere were riveted, sometimes welded, together to create two types of ships: the 1022 Type A freighter and the Type 1024 Type Troop Transport (more properly described as a cargo liner in that it had quite considerable cargo capacity). While the contract was for 180 ships, 110 of the former and twelve of the latter were constructed over four years but none were completed before 11 November 1918. The first was ss *Quistconck*, delivered on 3 December 1918. In 1941, she was purchased by the British Ministry of War Transport (MOWT) and renamed *Empire Falcon*, sailed in many convoys and was eventually scrapped in 1953 after thirty-five years of continual service. The shipyard closed in 1921 and the site eventually became Philadelphia International Airport.

Edward N Hurley who was Chairman of the USSB and who wrote the book *Bridge to France* in 1927, said in Chapter 7 that:

Theodore Ferris [Theodore E Ferris, Naval Architect and Chief Designer of the EFC] had justly earned for himself an enviable reputation as a naval architect, and to him must be given much of the credit for laying down the plans for the type of fabricated steel ship . . . Ferris produced the design of the fabricated ship which the Fleet Corporation built. Theodore Ferris would be the last man to claim credit for the idea of fabricating ships, although the Fleet Corporation owed much to him for carrying it into execution.

However, Ferris was not alone in his endeavours. While some 1,000 steel and timber ships became to be thought of as 'Ferris Ships', another naval architect, Daniel H Cox – a partner in the firm of Cox & Stevens – was in charge of the Department of Naval Architecture and Marine Engineering of the Fleet

Corporation and later of the Ship Construction Division. We shall hear more of Cox in Chapters 12 and 14.

Insofar as the Hog Island Type A was concerned, at least, function clearly took priority over appearance. They were singularly unattractive ships – the reverse of the 'all show and no go' saying. Ease of fabrication – up to 80 per cent was prefabricated – for mass production was a top priority and that meant simplifying anything and everything possible. However, far less corners were cut than the British N class. There would seem to have been no cross-pollination or transfer of technology here. Or, if there was, the British 'cut-to-the-bone' approach was

discounted. Perhaps the Americans were looking to the future – to how, where and to what use these ships might be put after hostilities. In this regard they were more prescient. Many Hog Islanders went on to serve in and through the Second World War. Similar to the N class, the ships had no sheer and no camber to the decks. The decks were absolutely parallel to the water, the bow plumb. The Type B even had a plumb stern and was so symmetrical that in silhouette and from a distance it was impossible to determine bow from stern. This was a deliberate ploy to confuse submarines and had been tried in a number of British ships such as the '24'-class minesweeping sloops which

HOG ISLAND TYPE 'A'
EFC DESIGN 1022

America's answer to prefabricated ships arrived too late but served on into the Second World War in various guises.

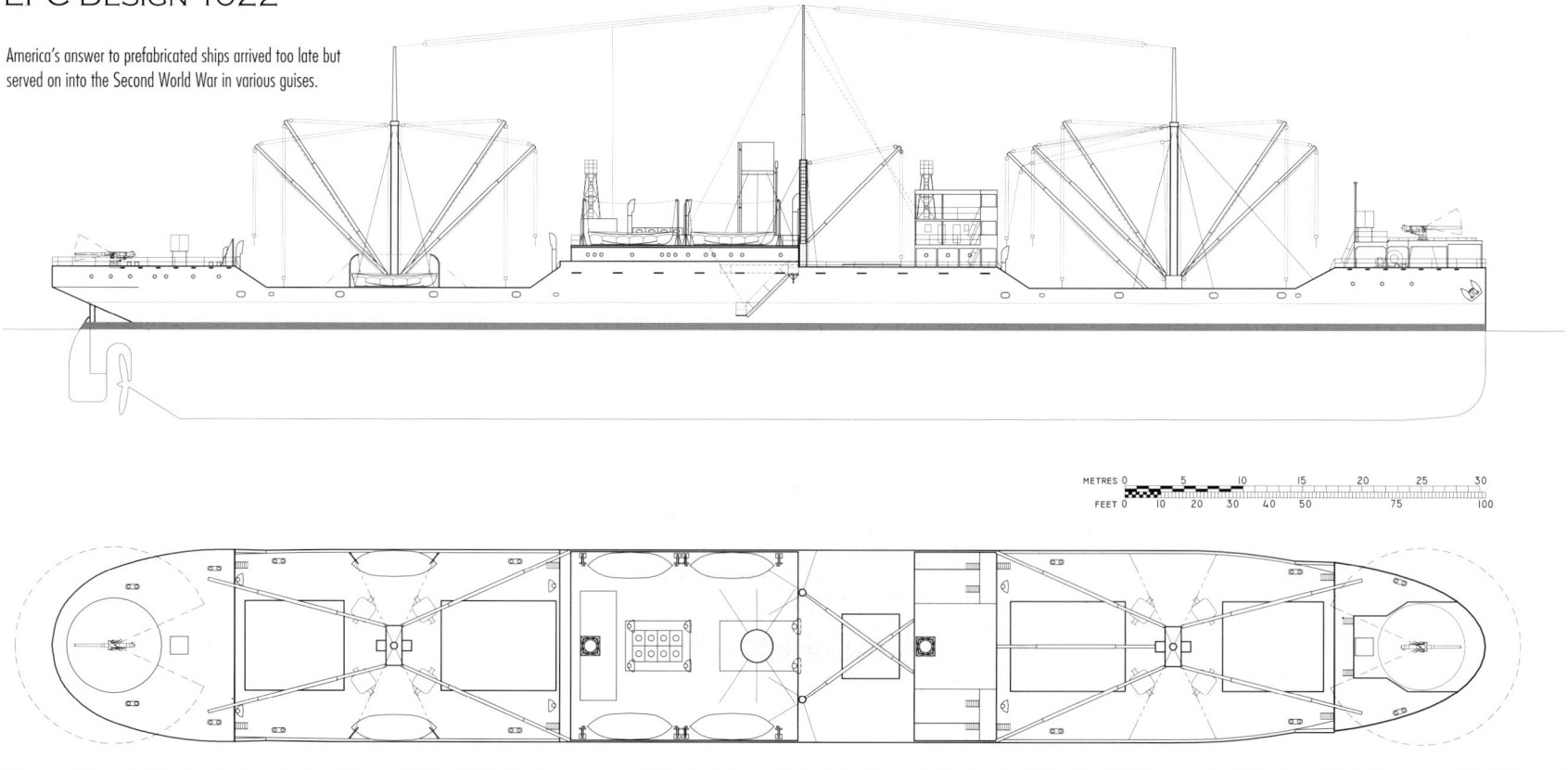

| METRES | 0 | 5 | 10 | 15 | 20 | 25 | 30 |
| FEET | 0 | 10 | 20 | 30 | 40 | 50 | 75 | 100 |

A Hog Island Type A. Note the complete absence of sheer to the hull. (shipscribe.com)

USS *Sirius*, a Hog Island Type A in service with the USN as a cargo ship. (Naval History & Heritage Command NH 67872)

even had fake anchors at the stern. Both Type A and B Classes were double-ended with parallel sides and, surprisingly, considerable overhang and flair at the bow and stern. One would have thought that, in the interests of simplicity (less curved plating to be furnaced, formed, fitted and perhaps re-furnaced and the process repeated) this could have been reduced to a more pointed plan shape with flat plating. Unlike the N class, they had conventional rounded (soft) bilges. Again, and surprisingly, instead of simple reciprocating machinery (quick and easy to build and operate), double-reduction geared turbines to a single shaft were chosen and oil-fired boilers were used. The Type As were capable of 11 knots and the Type Bs, 15 knots.

CHAPTER 5: BETWEEN THE WARS

After the war, war-built tonnage mainly re-equipped the world's merchant fleets so there was little demand between the wars for new shipping. The British Government's 'Scrap-and-Build' initiatives – that is, replacing one ton of old for one ton of new – and low-cost Government finance or low-interest/high-ratio loans but no scrapping eased some of the pain to shipbuilders. Booms and slumps were the natural order of things in shipbuilding. The world no longer wanted warships and there were too many war-built merchant ships going cheaply. Rising costs and lower output placed British yards at a double disadvantage, reducing their ability to secure orders. The industry reached its lowest ebb as the 1930s began. Things began to pick up in 1936–7 and despite some lean years, some yard closures and company amalgamations, in 1939 all British shipyards had full order books – either from naval orders, merchant shipping or both. Small shipyards, used to building to mercantile standards and with slipways limited in size, found themselves in the unusual situation of undertaking Admiralty orders for the new 'Flower'-class corvettes: fifty-six in July–August 1939 plus another seventy-five immediately after September 1939. Other orders were placed in France and Canada to cope with demand.

The United States responded in a different way and for different reasons. In 1936 the United States Maritime Commission (USMC) was formed as part of the Maritime Act. Part of President Roosevelt's New Deal, it was a government agency devised to reverse the general decline of the United States Merchant Marine and reverse the decline in shipbuilding after the demise of the USSB and the EFC. Its mandate was '. . . to develop and maintain a Merchant Marine sufficient to carry a substantial portion of the water-borne export and import foreign commerce of the United States on the best-equipped, safest and most suitable type of vessels owned, operated and constructed by citizens of the United States, manned with a trained personnel and capable of serving as a naval and military auxiliary in time of war or national emergency'.

A document produced in 1940 by the USMC entitled 'America Builds Ships: The Program of the United States Maritime Commission', is a simple-to-read publication with the minimum of explanation and maximum of word-pictures to get the simple message across in some sixty pages. Quoting from it, it states that an economic survey of the American marine found (in 1937) that 'of the American fleet of 1,422 ocean going vessels (of 2,000 tons and over), 91.8 per cent will be obsolete by 1942. This fleet represents 8,407,000 gross tons. Of the tonnage, 88 per cent will be obsolete by 1942.' A page of basic silhouettes showed the nine types to be built then, under the heading 'Why a Building Program?', the answer provided was that 'Different types of ships are needed for varied services required by shippers and travellers. More than 150 of these nine types have been ordered. The minimum goal is 500 ships in ten years.' Interestingly, a following drawing entitled, 'United States Builds Better and Safer Ships', shows a theoretical ship captioned as follows (stern to bow): emergency steering gear, capstan for docking, cargo handling gear, cargo winch, automatic watertight doors, ventilator for holds, watertight bulkheads, modern lifeboats and equipment, fireproof materials in housing, fire-extinguishing equipment, gyroscopic compass, gyro pelorus repeater stands, elevator, modern radio equipment, radio direction finder, fathometer blinker lights and anchor windlass.

The US-flagged merchant ships were, on average, nearing the end of their commercial life and scrapped ships were not being replaced. The EFC had erred in having over fifty 'standard' designs. What the USMC felt was needed was a much smaller series of new standard designs and that these ships would be owned by the Commission and leased on a bareboat basis to the shipping companies. If shipping companies ordered their own ships, they had to be to those standard designs set by the

C 3

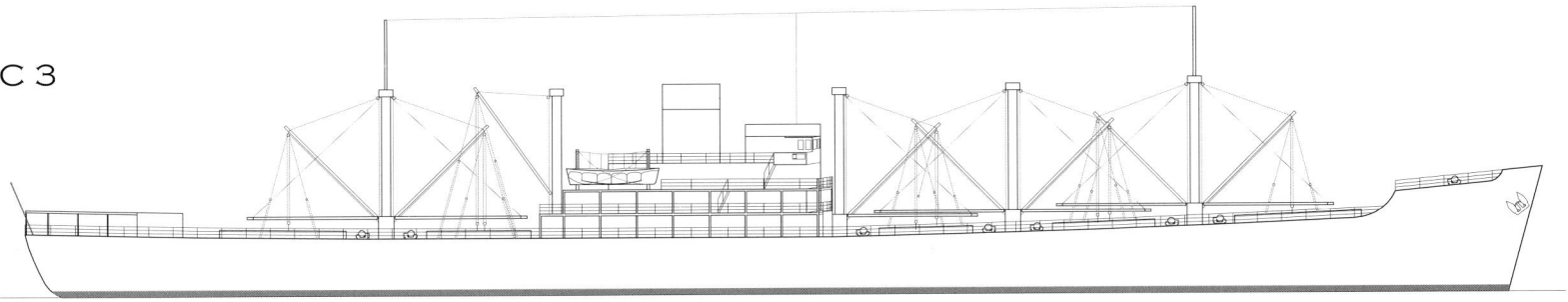

C 2

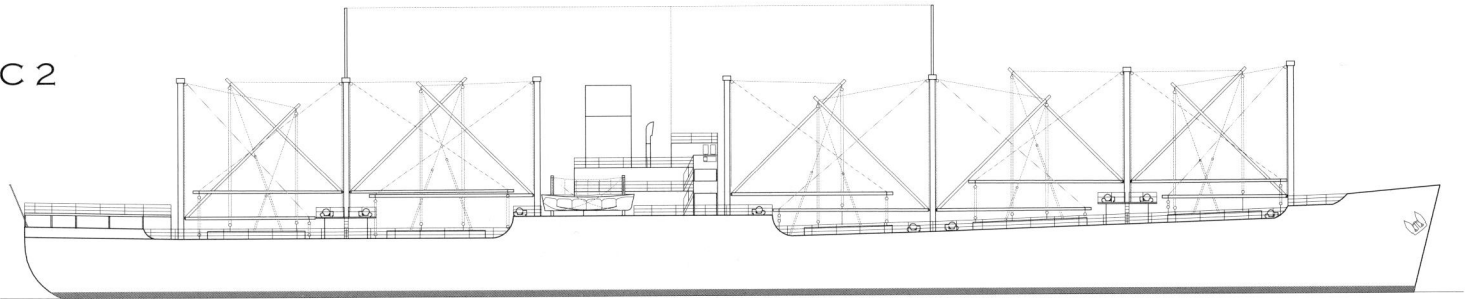

C 1 B

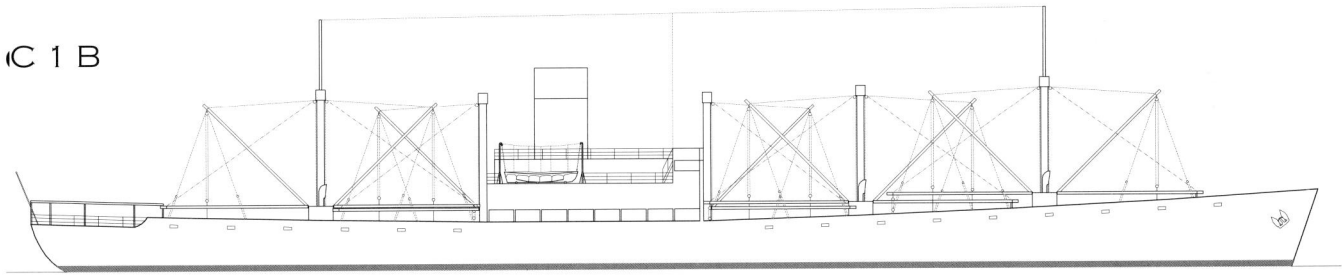

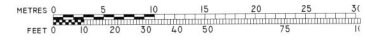

C 1 M

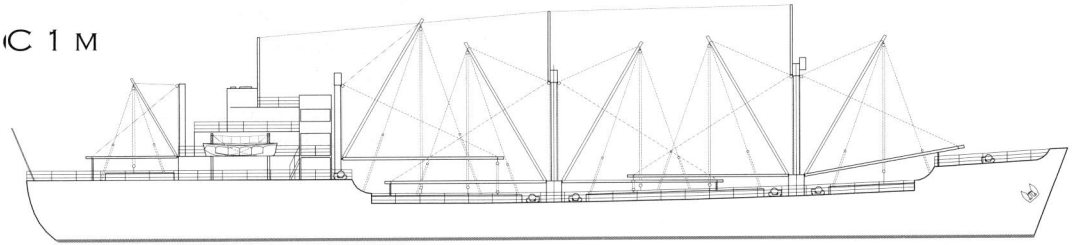

UNITED STATES MARITIME
COMMISSION SHIP TYPES

Commission or with variations approved by the Commission. In addition, Federal subsidies were made available for the construction and the operation of Merchant Marine vessels. Ships operating on routes in direct competition with foreign shipping could apply for a subsidy to cover the extra operating costs but only if the route was of strategic value plus the owners planned to replace older ships with new American-built ones. These ships would be subsidised by an amount equal to the difference in construction costs with foreign yards but the process and the ship plans had to be approved by the Maritime Commission.

Initially, there were three basic classes of cargo ships, as follows: C1: up to 400ft LOA, C2: 400–450ft LOA, C 3: over 450ft LOA. The C2 and C3 types were designed to be state-of-the-art ships: oil-fired, water-tube boilers, turbine-driven, welded construction and capable of speeds varying between 15.5 and 16.5 knots – all the things that the British equivalents, generally, were not. The C1 category was divided, ultimately, into four sub-classes: two were turbine-driven or diesel driven (C-1A and C1-B), one only turbine-driven (C1S-AY1) and one (C1-M and sub-types) only diesel-driven. The four basic types are shown in the drawing on page 25. Later, a T-2 tanker of 14.5–16 knots, and a C-4 cargo/troop transport capable of 17 knots were added. These have not been illustrated.

The standard types differed from older merchant ships in their use of high-speed turbine engines with double reduction gear, which allowed the ships to cruise at 15 knots no less efficiently than the existing 11-knot merchant ships, which mostly used reciprocating engines. The standard ships also had improved fireproofing, based on the experience of the *Morro Castle* disaster in September 1934. To attract men into the moribund Merchant Marine, crew accommodation was improved by moving quarters from the traditional forecastle to amidships and by supplying better basic facilities like hot and cold running water, better messrooms, improved ventilation and refrigeration.

Despite the fact that the United States had been pursuing a distinctly isolationist foreign policy, these ships were designed, built and organised in such a manner that they could be adapted as a naval auxiliary force in times of conflict. The USMC subsidised the extra costs involved.

Although there were only ten capable shipyards with some forty-six suitable-sized slipways between them, the broad aim was to produce fifty ships a year for ten years and train the requisite number of shipbuilders and merchant seaman along the way.

On 2 February 1942, Executive Order No 9054 established the War Shipping Administration (WSA) separating off from the USMC all but the shipbuilding responsibilities.

CHAPTER 6: BRITAIN 1940

The seven-month 'Phoney War' or 'Sitzkrieg' that followed Germany's invasion of Poland on 1 September 1939 ended with its invasion of Denmark and Norway in April 1940 and Belgium, the Netherlands, Luxembourg and France in May. At the end of May into early June, the British Expeditionary Force was successfully evacuated from Dunkirk. Italy entered the war as a member of the Axis on 10 June. France surrendered on 22 June. In July Germany launched the first of the prolonged air attacks that became the Battle of Britain. On 27 September Germany, Italy and Japan signed the Tripartite Pact, creating the Axis Alliance.

Britain was alone – an island off the shore of what had become, in effect, Nazi Europe – and dependent on its survival on its merchant fleet and those of its allies and, to some extent, those neutral nations prepared to run the gauntlet of German submarines and surface raiders in the Atlantic and the North Sea.

In 1939 Britain had, by far, the largest merchant fleet in the world, as below:

	SHIPS		TONS	
UK	6,722	29.65%	17,891,134	31.11%
USA	2,345	10.34%	8,909,892	15.49%
Japan	1,609	7.10%	5,996,607	10.43%
Norway	1,987	8.76%	4,833,813	8.41%
Germany	2,459	10.85%	4,482,662	7.79%
Italy	1,227	5.41%	3,424,804	5.96%
British Commonwealth*	2,255	9.95%	3,110,791	5.41%
Netherlands	1,523	6.72%	2,969,578	5.16%
France	1,231	5.43%	2,933,933	5.10%
Greece	607	2.68%	1,780,666	3.10%
Denmark	705	3.11%	1,174,944	2.04%
TOTALS	22,670	100%	57,508,824	100%

In February 1940, all shipbuilding and all ship repairing activity was placed under the direct control of the Admiralty. A Controller of Merchant Shipbuilding and Repairs sat on the Board of the Admiralty and an Advisory Committee of Merchant Shipbuilding reported to him. Ships could only be built either on orders of the Admiralty or, for private owners, under licences that required the ships to be built to Admiralty specifications of wartime requirements. The first thing this committee did was to standardise the ships being built in British shipyards so that they were no longer being built to the requirements of individual shipowners. This was done in order to make the best use of the scarce materials available, to reduce waste to the absolute minimum and to maximise the efficiency of the skilled workforce under increasingly difficult circumstances.

There were two basic standard designs: X and Y, although the Y developed over time into Y1, Y2, Y3, Y4, Y5, Y6 and Y7 versions due to minor variations in superstructure. The X Type all appear to have been 448ft LOA, 432–433ft LBP and 56ft beam and around 6,900–7,000 gross tons with diesel engines. Thirteen were built. The Y Type all appear to have been of similar dimensions, 446–448ft LOA, but with three-cylinder VTE engines. Tonnages varied between 7,000 (Y1) and 7,200 (Y7). Forty-six were built, of all types. Interestingly, and assessed purely from an appearance point of view, the Y Type, at least as exemplified by the Y7 shown in the photograph, more closely resembled a Liberty ship than the tramp or shelter-deck type that, ultimately, became the prototype hull and machinery for the Liberty ship. Also, the sort of construction economies of the transom stern were never adopted in the Liberty ship.

Of the many types of ships being built in British shipyards it

* Combined figure for all the Commonwealth countries.
No figures are available for the USSR.
Source: J Ellis, *The World War II Databook*.

was quickly decided that ships of the tramp type in the 9,000–10,0000 TDW capacity with LBP of 425ft and a beam of 56ft was the most appropriate although the depth of the ship should be increased. These ships were to be known as the Type PF (A) – the PF standing for prefabricated because that method of construction – at least in part – together with standardisation, was to be preferred as offering the best solution to delivering the necessary ships quickly and economically. Because the size of prefabricated units tended to be too large for most shipyards to handle, this design was never put into production. In its place, the PF (B) design was substituted involving smaller prefabricated units. In this design, the sheer was reduced to the very ends. Also, there was a greater distance between the bridge superstructure and the funnel and between the funnel and the kingposts serving Hold No 3 which also had twin derricks. One 30-ton, two 10-ton and eight 5-ton derricks were fitted and hatchways were later made larger to accommodate heavier and bulkier cargoes with 50-ton derricks to suit. The PF (B) type were 446ft LOA, 431ft LBP, 56ft beam, 7,060 gross tons, three-cylinder VTE engine, 10–11 knots. Forty-one were built.

The PF (C) Type combined the superstructure in one, placing Holds 1, 2 and 3 forward of the bridge with one 50-ton, five 10-ton and five 5-ton derricks, all better able to handle bulky and heavy deck-cargoes. The PF (C) type were 448ft LOA, 431ft

LBP, 7,300 gross tons, 3-cylinder VTE engine, 10–11 knots. Thirteen were built.

The PD (D) Type was similar to the C Type. Both had angular, V-shaped transom sterns for economy of construction but the D Type had a raised poop for additional accommodation. Eight were built. Mitchel & Sawyer also refer to a Type R of which nine were built and which measured 421ft LOA, 406ft LBP, 54ft beam, 6,140–6,209 gross tons, and had three-cylinder VTE engines.

There was also a total of 145 similar-sized ships from fifteen different builders that no Type are ascribed to, despite the fact that some of these builders built one or more or the prescribed Types and despite the fact that the ships fall within the range of length, beam and tonnage. It must be assumed, therefore, that these were not of the standardised types but to the builders' own standard type. There were twenty-four cargo liners and refrigerated ships varying between 8,563 and 13,478 tons, ten 'Bel'-type (7,500–7,800 tons) and ten 'Empire Malta'-type (3,540 tons) heavy lift ships, sixty-one 'Scandinavian'-type (three-island design, 2,900 tons) and sixty-eight large tankers in three classes varying between 8,100 and 9,900 tons, plus a plethora of smaller tankers, coasters, colliers, tugs and ferries.[1] The reason that these vessels do not form part of this book is that not being of the tramp or shelter-deck type they had no part to play in the lineage of the Liberty ship.

CHAPTER 7: THE BATTLE OF THE ATLANTIC 1939-1945

On 3 September 1939, Britain's Prime Minister, Neville Chamberlain, broadcast to the nation the fact that a state of war existed with Germany as a result of Germany's invasion of Poland and Britain and France's alliance with Poland. The Second World War had begun.

Nine hours later the transatlantic liner *Athenia* was torpedoed 250 miles north-west of Ireland by the German submarine *U-30* with the loss of 117 lives. German U-boats had been deployed ahead of the commencement of hostilities. The intention was clear. And so, commenced the Battle of the Atlantic; a battle that lasted 2,073 relentless days – just short of six years – until peace was signed on 7 May 1945. Prime Minister Churchill is believed to have coined the term and later wrote that 'The only thing that ever really frightened me during the war was the U-boat peril'. He also wrote the Battle of the Atlantic was '…the dominating factor all through the war. Never for one moment could we forget that everything happening elsewhere, on land, at sea, or in the air, depended ultimately on its outcome'.

Unlike other specific campaigns of the European war – The Battle of France, the Dunkirk Evacuation, the Norwegian Campaign, the North Africa Campaign, the Battle of Britain, the Invasion of Europe, to mention but a few – the Battle of the Atlantic occupied the whole of the period of the war, without respite. It was a battle that simply had to be won. It was, in its very essence, the difference between failure and success, the difference between Britain surviving or being subjugated by Germany.

Britain, an island nation, relied heavily on its trade routes to export its manufactured goods and to import its raw materials and foodstuffs. No other country was so vitally dependent on seaborne trade. Sir Henry Newbolt summed it up in his poem '*The King's Highway*'. The trade routes were just that – the King's Highway. The Empire's Highway. Recognising this, in the First World War, Germany tried to starve Britain into submission through a then-novel U-boat-centred blockade of the Atlantic trade routes. Germany was in turn blockaded by the Royal Navy in the North Sea, denying the German High Seas Fleet access to these sea lanes. Historians are divided as to whether the blockade ultimately brought Germany to its knees and precipitated the November revolution which led to the collapse of the Kaiser's government and his exile.

While Britain had the world's largest merchant fleet in 1939 – 6,722 ships totalling 17,891,134 tons – losses to its fleet and the fleets of its allies, primarily via Germany's U-boat campaign and also via its commerce raider campaign, exceeded than its ability to replace the lost ships. Had that downward spiral continued unabated, Britain would have reached the point where it would not be able to maintain the level of materiel necessary to conduct the war and to feed its people. The end result of that is self-evident.

The Royal Navy defended these vital shipping lanes by immediately reverting to the lesson learnt in the last eighteen months of the First World War of assembling merchant ships into convoys, defended by as many escorts – mainly fleet destroyers at first – as could be spared. Convoys had proven their value in the Age of Sail with the concentration of and economy of force to ward off pirates and privateers. In Napoleonic times, marine insurers demanded a War Risks Premium one-third to one-half greater for ships sailing independently.

In the vast expanses of the Atlantic Ocean, one large convoy is harder to find than, say, the forty-odd individual ships it might contain all sailing independently on a similar route. Forty such ships are forty times more likely to be discovered than one. Given that a convoy might take between fifteen and twenty days for an Atlantic crossing, depending on speed and the evasive route taken, and that there was about one sailing a week, there might be between ten and twenty convoys spread over an immense ocean at any given time and the chances of detection were quite small.

Throughout the Battle, independently-routed ships accounted for the largest proportion of sinkings. While some convoys suffered

Rare German aerial reconnaissance photo of Convoy PQ-17 underway for Murmansk, taken before 4 July 1942 when the ill-fated convoy was dispersed. The silhouettes of some of the six Liberty ships in the convoy can be discerned in the original. (Naval History & Heritage Command NH 71382)

grievously – particularly when whole wolf-packs of U-boats made contact and attacked *en masse* – the vast majority of transatlantic convoys arrived at their destinations intact. This may have been as high as 91.57 per cent depending on how you interpret the many tables in Hague's excellent work, *The Allied Convoy System 1939-1945*. However, what can be deduced from the data is that something in the order of 96,000 merchant ships were convoyed in an average convoy size of thirty ships for a loss ratio of less than 1.0 per cent.

While a convoy was a method of saving ships, it was also a method of destroying submarines. A convoy forced the opponent to come to it and accordingly gave the escorts opportunities to attack the submarines. Sinking them was not the escorts' stated objective – at least not until such time in the Battle of the Atlantic as the numbers of escorts available allowed this luxury. Until then, the object was, 'The safe and timely arrival of the convoy' and to achieve this the escorts were to keep the submarines submerged where their inferior speed and range under electric power made them less of a threat.

The Battle of the Atlantic can be divided into seven relatively distinct periods.

1. **September 1939 to June 1940** was marked by submerged daylight attacks on independent merchantmen. While the German U-boat fleet was small, the escort force available to the RN was also small and convoys were thinly protected and there were insufficient escorts to accompany convoys beyond 100 nautical miles west of Ireland. After two or three days' sailing, outbound convoys dispersed following independent routes. Inbound convoys were met a similar distance from Ireland. It would not be until much later in the battle that a port-to-port convoy defence would be available as more escorts – particularly 'Flower'-class corvettes – became available. Submarine attacks were conventional: daylight at periscope depth and directed at the large number of merchant ships that were travelling independently or stragglers from convoys.

2. **July 1940 to March 1941** was marked by a change of tactics

and saw night attacks on the surface against convoys. The fall of France allowed German long-range reconnaissance aircraft to patrol well out into the Atlantic and direct U-boats to convoys. Basing U-boats in French Atlantic ports considerably shortened transit times allowing more times for patrol. From September 1939 to July 1940, the ratio of U-boats in service to U-boats at sea was 2.35:1. From July 1940 to July 1941, the ratio of U-boats in service to U-boats at sea was 1.84:1 – an improvement of almost 22 per cent. The threat on invasion diverted RN ships that would have escorted transatlantic convoys from the Western Approaches to the south of England. June 1940 to February 1941 was known by the German submariners as 'The Happy Time'. Convoys were shadowed in daylight and attacked on the surface at night, U-boats often entering the columns of the convoys.

3. **April 1941 to December 1941** was marked by the increasing use of wolf-pack attacks and by the evasive routing of British convoys. Instead of individual night attacks on the surface, wolf packs became the norm. When a convoy was contacted, instead of attacking immediately, the wolf pack was directed to the convoy so that by acting in concert the escort would be overwhelmed. At this time, the average number of escorts available to a convoy was only five. The new building

Atlantic convoy off Newfoundland, 28 July 1942. Note the large number of tankers. (Naval History & Heritage Command 80-G-21187)

programme had been accelerated and about twenty U-boats were being commissioned each month. Fortunately, the threat of invasion having been removed, largely due to Hitler's shift to the East and Operation 'Barbarossa', more escort ships became available and shore-based aircraft equipped with air-to-surface radar began to have an impact. Convoys became larger and more sophisticated in their routing with port-to-port escorts, the first of which occurred in May 1941.

4. **January 1942 to September 1942** was marked by attacks along the American eastern seaboard. America's entry into the war gave Germany the opportunity to direct its U-boat activity against an unprepared foe. Admiral Ernest King, Commander-in-Chief of the United States Fleet, and an Anglophobe, would not accept the Royal Navy doctrine of convoys and persisted in allowing unescorted shipping and refused the loan of Royal Navy escort vessels. Losses were catastrophic – 698,000 gross tons in June alone when the convoy system was finally adopted. The Germans called it the 'Second Happy Time'. U-boats sank ships faster than they were being built until about the end of 1942. Losses began to be reduced as convoy and other measures were introduced. Among these was an increased use of High-Frequency Direction-Finding (HF/DF, 'Huff Duff') which allowed 105 out of 174 North Atlantic convoys to be diverted away from ambushes and for twenty-three convoys to partially avoid them. Sixteen were not so fortunate, however. Lack of targets saw German attention was redirected south to the less well-defended soft spots, the Caribbean and Gulf of Mexico.

5. **October 1942 to June 1943** was marked by large wolf packs attacking convoys in the north-west Atlantic. The mid-ocean gap – that part of the North Atlantic that was not covered by very long-range (VLR) land-based aircraft – became the focus of the U-boats in October 1942 and large wolf packs spread out in patrol lines covering vast expanses of the ocean with up to 100 U-boats at sea. Concerted attacks disorganised convoy formations and their defence. Trade tonnage lost in November topped 700,000 gross tons. May 1943 saw a turning point, however, as more VLR aircraft became available, and escort aircraft carriers sailed in support of convoys. Also, the average number of escorts available to a convoy had risen to eight. Convoy ONS 5 (outward bound, Britain to USA) saw a decisive battle with six U-boats sunk and seven damaged of the fifty-eight ranged against it. After 17 May, no ships were sunk in the North Atlantic for some time.

6. **July 1943 to May 1944** was marked by a temporary abandonment of the large wolf packs in the North Atlantic. The Germans sought to find a soft spot in Allied defences and failed. July saw more U-boats sunk than merchant ships for the first time in the Battle of the Atlantic. They were forced to stay submerged and were forced to adopt a defensive posture. They lost mobility but had some successes with acoustic torpedoes, especially against the escorts. Despite concentrated efforts, the Germans were unable to counter the Allies' technological superiority and their application of radar, HF/DF and the deployment of aircraft in the anti-submarine war.

7. **June 1944 to the end of the War** was marked by operations in British home waters. The D-Day invasion of Normandy saw an immediate requirement to redirect aggressive action in the English Channel but the heavy concentration of air and sea patrols meant there were only limited successes. In August and September, the U-boats were forced to withdraw from their French bases and had to be content with a coastal offensive in British waters which had only limited success. Production difficulties denied the Germans the use of the technically-advanced but unproven Type XXI U-boat and the surrender in May 1945 occurred before these became operational.

CHAPTER 8: JOSEPH L THOMPSON & SONS LTD, NORTH SANDS, SUNDERLAND

Joseph L Thompson & Sons Ltd's shipyard on the River Wear at North Sands, Sunderland probably in the late 1930s. Note the three ships under construction appear to be of the same shelter-deck type with two holds forward of the superstructure with a small hold forward of the boiler and engine room and two holds aft. Note also how cramped the shipyard is and how the ways are angled to the river. The North Sea is to the right of the photograph. (searlecanada.org)

Dating back to 1346 and once dubbed 'the largest shipbuilding town in the world', Sunderland on the River Wear, a Municipal Borough of County Durham, sported no less than eight major shipbuilding companies at the beginning of the Second World War. However, back in 1840 there were no less than seventy-six shipbuilding yards building wooden ships, the last of which was built in 1880 by which time iron-hulled ships had taken over. This change resulted in smaller shipyards closing or amalgamating and the numbers reduced and yards became fewer, larger and more industrialised so that by the First World War there were sixteen yards in operation. Yards had come and gone during the boom-and-bust periods that

characterised the industry such as the downturns between 1884 and 1887 and 1908–10 and, of course, particularly the Great Depression of the 1930s.

The shipyard of Robert Thompson & Sons was founded in 1846 and became Joseph L Thompson in 1871. It was during the 1930s slump that Thompson's used the slack time to conduct research work aimed at gaining an advantage when the economy improved. It was aimed at improving their own construction methods but also providing a better product: a cheaper, 10,000-ton cargo-carrying ship with better performance that was also economic to operate.

At the beginning of the twentieth century, Britain was the world leader in ship design – not just with the advent of the Dreadnought battleship but in commercial ships also. The majority of the world's commercial shipping was built in Britain's shipyards. Notwithstanding, the industry was subject to fluctuation of supply and demand. The excess of shipping built during the closing stages of the First World War, particularly in the United States, took a long time to absorb although the Government 'Scrap & Build' and low interest loan initiatives helped somewhat. Thompson's went through a lean period – with no launches whatsoever in the period 1931–4. Robert Cyril Thompson (usually called Cyril), in charge of Thompson's drawing office, used the National Physical Laboratory's testing tanks at Teddington to test models with different hull forms. The traditional fine entry with a plumb stem and a full stern was reversed to give a fuller entry (about 45°) with a raked bow and finer lines leading into the stern post with a cruiser or cutaway stern. Rudders, instead of trailing completely behind the rudder post were semi-balanced – that is, with a portion (up to 20 per cent of the rudder area) ahead of the rudder post) offering less drag when the ship was under helm.

North-Eastern Marine Engineering Co Ltd (NEMEC), also

of Sunderland (founded 1860 and closed in 1982), designed an improved VTE engine. This was a re-heater type and had been first advertised by NEMEC in 1926. It achieved extra fuel economy by use of a re-heater which raised the temperature of the steam as it passed from the high pressure to the intermediate pressure cylinders by leading it via a chamber heated by steam coming direct from boiler maintaining it in a super-heated condition.

None of these improvements can be attributed solely to Cyril Thompson. None were completely new. But it was Thompson who put them all together, combining all the attributes into one ship – the SS *Embassage*, Hull No 572, launched on 31 July 1935

and completed in September for Hall Brothers Steamship Co. of nearby Newcastle. *Embassage* was not revolutionary, she was evolutionary but was nonetheless a milestone in ship design. Unfortunately, details as to her dimensions are imprecise. Elphick merely states a 9,100 deadweight.[1] Lloyd's Register gives *Embassage* as 409.2ft x 57.6ft x 24.0ft with 4,954 GRT. This tonnage accords with the Hall List register.[2]

I managed to sight a drawing from the Tyne and Wear Archives and Museum entitled: 'ss. EMBASSAGE, S.S. No. 572 (which is Thompson's Hull Number) 400'0" BP, x 57'8" EXT, x 35'3½" MLD, UPPER DK, 57'4½" MLD x 27'0½" MLD 2nd DK, COMPLETE STRUCTURE TYPE, Scale: 1/8" = 1'.' It

The only known drawing to exist of SS *Embassage* and held by the Tyne & Wear Archives and Museum. Note the raked bow, the cut-away forefoot and the rudder of the balanced type with a portion of its area ahead of the vertical pivot point with the trailing edge parallel to the pivot point – not curved as was common at the time. (Tyne & Wear Archives & Museums)

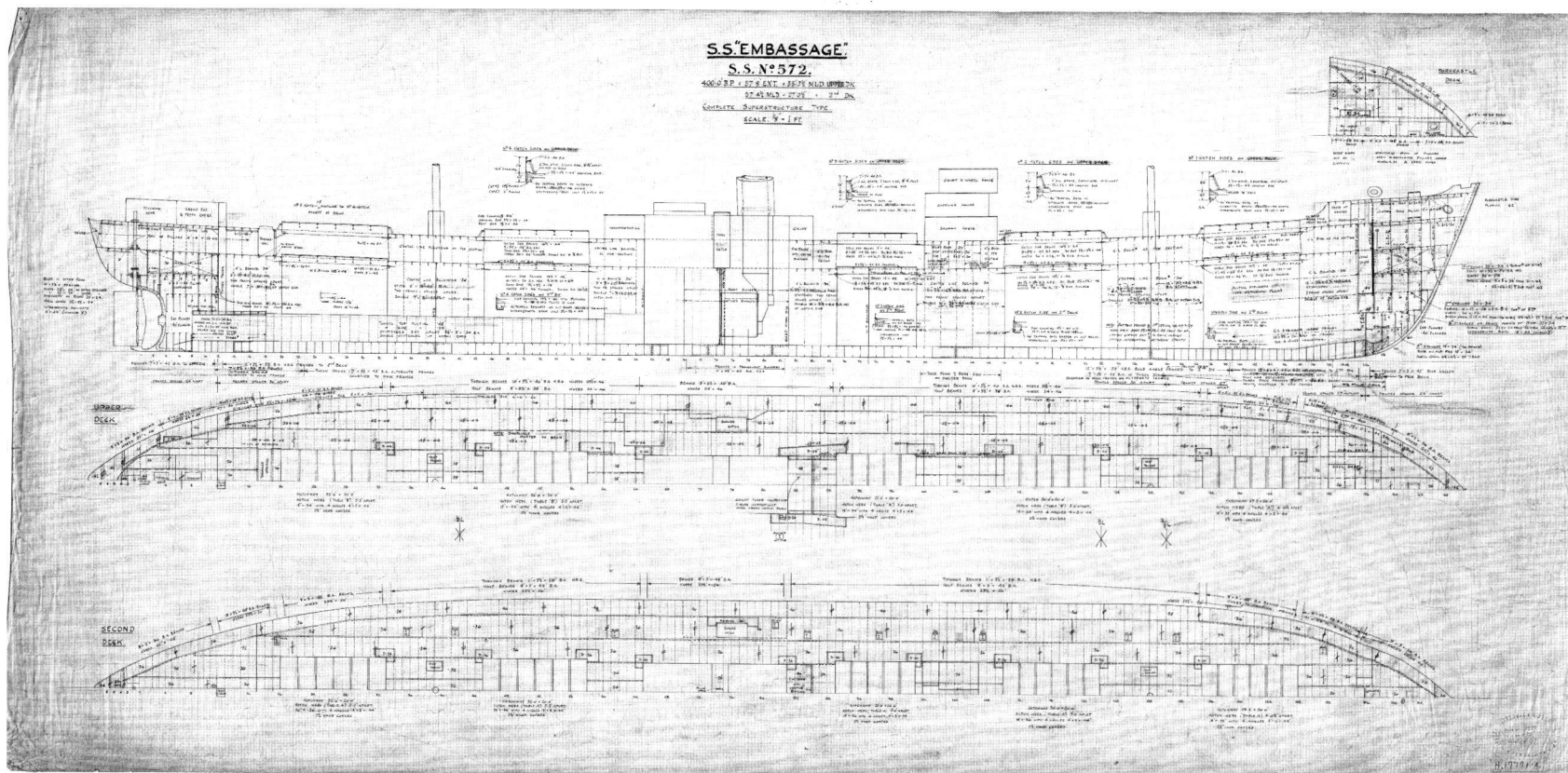

SS *Embassage*. The fountainhead; without this ship there would have been no Liberty ship as we know it. (City of Vancouver Archives CVA 447-2184)

had an oval stamp at the bottom right-hand corner that was faint but the words could just be made out in the border: 'Joseph L Thompson & Sons Limited, Sunderland'. Within the stamp, besides the printed words 'Plan No., Ship No. and Date' were the handwritten numbers; 10239, 572 and 28/1/35 respectively. The drawing was highly detailed – to all intents and purposes, what would be for a building called a structural drawing, in that it details all of the structural components, their sizes, types, spacings and fixings. There were even small detail drawings within the main drawing that amplified items. This drawing would have to be interpreted in conjunction with the other drawings showing the ship's lines and the various sections or frames. It is unfortunate that it is the only drawing remaining. Note that Thompson's drawing gives a 400ft 0in B.P. whereas the Lloyd's register quotes 409.2ft (see earlier). I cannot account for this sort of discrepancy but this was by no means the only one I was to discover in my search for Liberty's provenance.

A beautifully detailed model at 1/96 scale (1in to the foot) was made at the time *Embassage* was either proposed or under construction and was sold by the Vallejo Gallery in 2007. Eight coloured photographs can be found at vallejogallery.com and these were used to help develop my drawing which follows. The model builder's plate states that the ship was 428ft 0in LOA and 57ft 8in beam. Again, a different set of dimensions.

Her reheated VTE engine of 1,500 IHP had cylinders of 21½in, 37in and 62in and a stroke of 42in, operated at 220 psi and developed 353 NHP (Lloyd's Register). She used 16–17 tons of coal per day instead of the customary 25 tons at 10 knots for a ship of that size and tonnage. The cost was a competitive £95,000.

Embassage led to further orders. Hall Brothers Steamship Co. must have been justifiably pleased with the ship because they ordered *Royal Sceptre* from Thompson's (Hull No 583, launched 20 November 1937, completed December 1937) which was 431ft 8in (presumably LOA) x 58.2ft x 24.8ft and 4,853 GRT (sunderlandships.com) and there may have been others before an order from the Hall Brothers Steamship Co. for Hull No 592 which became *Dorington Court* for the London-based Court Line

bridge which were more of a danger to the users than they were to enemy aircraft. As more and better weapons became available, the number of Oerlikons grew with additional mountings replacing the Lewis guns and also in bandstands forward and at the aft end of the boat deck (see *Ocean Vanguard* drawing, previous chapter and drawings of 'Fort' types, Chapter 15).

Empire Liberty was sold to the Greek government in 1943 and became *Kyklades*, according to *Shipbuilding and Shipping Record* 1942. It seems odd that a publication dated 1942 could report on an event that happened in 1943! In 1947 she was sold and became *Mentor* and was scrapped in Osaka, Japan in 1960.[1] But *Empire Liberty*'s story does not end here, insofar as this book is concerned.

COMPARISON TABLE

	EMBASSAGE	DORINGTON COURT		EMPIRE WAVE HULL #607	EMPIRE LIBERTY HULL #611	OCEAN VANGUARD	LIBERTY SHIP
SOURCE	Lloyd's Register	Lloyd's Register	Bourneuf	As above	As above	Bourneuf	Accepted fact
LAUNCHED	31 Jul 1935	7 Mar 1939	n/a	28 Mar 1941	23 Aug 1941	16 Aug 1941	27 Sep 1941
LOA	428ft 0in (model)	443ft 6in	n/a	439ft 0in (Lloyd's Register)	441ft 0in	441ft 6in	441ft 6in
LBP	409.20ft	426ft 0in	416ft 0in	424ft 0in	416ft 0in	416ft 0in	416ft 0in
BEAM	57ft 6in/57ft 8in Lloyd's/Model	59.9ft	59ft 3in	60ft 0in	57ft 2in	57ft 0in	57ft 0in
DRAFT	24.00ft	25ft 6in	24ft 9½in	n/a	25ft 6in	26ft 11in	26ft 10in
GRT	4,954	5,281	n/a	7,463	7,157	7,157	7,176
DWT	9,100			10,000 (nominal)	10,000 (nominal)	10,100	10,414 (as planned)

Note: Lloyd's Register use a mixture of feet and inches and feet and decimal feet.

CHAPTER 11: THE 'OCEANS' AND HENRY J KAISER

The Merchant Shipbuilding Mission needed an opportunist like Henry J Kaiser to see the potential of an order for sixty ships rather than the problem that such an order seemed to present to the other shipyards the mission had visited. To Kaiser 'Problems are only opportunities in work clothes.'

The first meeting with Kaiser took place on 23 October 1940 – twenty days after the Mission's arrival – at Kaiser's Portland, Oregon facility. Kaiser headed a West Coast group (The Six Companies, Inc) plus Bath Iron Works (Maine) and Todd Shipyards Corporation (Texas). That meeting was followed shortly after by a second, more important meeting in Oakland, California. While Kaiser's shipbuilding was not his main strength, the mission fully understood that in order to fulfil an order for sixty ships, new facilities would need to be constructed and Kaiser's record in civil engineering works – the Boulder Dam, the San Francisco–Oakland Bridge, the Colorado River Aqueduct and railway projects – made that combination with existing shipbuilding via the Kaiser-Todd shipyard in Seattle, and the Bath Iron Works (also a shipyard) a potentially viable proposition. The cost of establishing those shipyards was just going to have to be amortised over the sixty ships – an unwelcome but unfortunate reality.

C J Tassava's thesis for his doctorate puts a different emphasis on just how this important meeting took place (Chapter 3). He states that Admiral H L Vickery, Land's second-in-command, asked the president of the Los Angeles-based Consolidated Steel Corporation for a recommendation for an organisation capable of fulfilling the British order and the Six Companies was put forward. This apparently suited Land because he wanted to split the order equally between the East and West Coast and there is more than a strong suggestion that in doing so, and not detracting from the USMC's programme, that when the British order was completed, there would be additional contracts available from that programme. The yards by then would had

been built with British capital, would be paid for and be an asset of the shipbuilding consortium costing them nothing. It was logical to get the most use out of the facilities and switch seamlessly over to USMC orders.

Whichever way it was orchestrated, meetings were held, negotiations took place and a deal-in-principle was struck. Unfortunately, we don't know what date or exactly the details of the negotiations or the deal. It appears that it was organised by the end of October or early November – just when the Presidential election was coming to a head – and that the necessary approval from the US Government was either forthcoming or that matters proceeded on the understanding that the approval was a formality only. Certainly, a Report on Preliminary Purchase Negotiation was submitted by the British Purchasing Commission and went before the US Treasury Department on 13 November with Admiral Land's backing. The estimated value of the deal was then £24 million (£400,000 per ship) of which almost 10 per cent was for the two new shipyards – in effect the premium the British were paying. But it was a sellers' market.

While the finer points of the deal are not known, the mechanics of what was to be built are well known. Elphick states that Hull No 607, later *Empire Wave* (seventh in the batch of ten, *Empire Wind* being the first – see Appendix C) was used as the basis of the order.[1] Because Kaiser's preferred method of construction was by welding, the working drawings and specifications had to be amended. This was no small undertaking and the New York naval architects of Gibbs & Cox were engaged – presumably at the consortium's expense – to assist the process originally commenced by Thompson and the Todd drawing office. I will make reference to the matter of ships' drawings several times in this book.

Riveted construction was regarded as old-fashioned by the Americans. It required skilled tradesmen who developed that skill over many years. Riveting required teamwork with rivets having to be heated to just the right temperature, thrown and caught then placed in specially aligned holes with one man forcing the rivet through from the outside of the ship while a two-man team hammered the rivet into a dome-shape on the inside – or one man used a pneumatic gun to do the same job. The rivet cooled and shrank giving a tight bond. However, welding could be taught 'on the job' and a competent welder could be fully trained in four months. Use could be made of a large, mobile and readily-available but largely unskilled workforce. Welding also saved steel and gave a smoother under-water surface. On the other hand, a riveted ship was more rigid and had less 'give'. Welded ships tended to expand and contract on the slipways, causing problems such as when aligning propeller shafts.

Having resolved the issue of welding as opposed to riveting, the next specification to be addressed was that of propulsion. While oil-fired, water-tube boilers powering steam turbines were the then-preferred combination of the USMC, such a specification created four problems for the Mission. First, the inevitable delay in getting the turbines due to the heavy demands on the relatively few suppliers capable of making these complex pieces of machinery. Second, the relative unfamiliarity of the average British merchant engineering officer/seaman with turbines as compared with reciprocating engines. Third, the fact that Britain had to import all its oil yet exported coal so had a plentiful supply of the latter. Fourth, which went hand-in-hand with the others, was the relative simplicity and familiarity of the Scotch boilers as compared with water-tube boilers. One could argue that Harry Hunter might have had a vested interest in pushing for his NEMEC engines, but the fact remains that they were a well proven engine and it was not NEMEC that was to build them but, in this instance, the General Machinery Corporation based in Hamilton, Ohio. The proof of that pudding is that the same engine design went on to power all of the 'Ocean' class and the designs that flowed from it.

However, no sooner had the Treasury Department approval been sought and Thompson received advice from the Admiralty on 16 November 1940 of a change of requirements wanting, according to Elphick, more cargo-carrying capacity. I believe that Elphick is wrong here when he says that this is where *Empire Liberty* 'entered the story' indicating that in doing so, it met the

Admiralty requirements for more cargo-carrying capacity.[2] Hull No 607 (*Empire Wave*) that had, to that time, formed the basis, the working hypothesis for their negotiations, and was 439ft 0in LOA x 60ft 0in beam and 7,463 GRT whereas the later Hull No 611 (*Empire Liberty* and the first ship in the second batch of thirteen ships this time) (see Appendix C) was 441ft 0in LOA but 57ft 0in beam and only 7,157 GRT, some 306 tons less – not more! If the Admiralty required a change it was for some other reason that *Empire Liberty* was preferred. One difference I was able to note when searching photographs to use was that a photograph I found that was attributable to *Empire Moon* (Hull No 605 and part of the first batch of ten) and which shows her bow when converted to a CAM ship (see Chapter 17), it is obvious that she has a forecastle whereas *Empire Lawrence* (Hull No 609 of the same batch) does not. That suggests two things: either the photographs' sources are unreliable – a distinct possibility – or there were changes made to these ships during the run of production. It was known that the high forecastle made steering difficult when in ballast and there had been a marked trend to move any accommodation located there aft or amidships anyway.

Regardless of the reason, it created an unwanted, untimely and unnecessary problem for Cyril Thompson. While Thompson may have been able to alter the specification – either by marginal notes or having them retyped – he would not have had the facilities to make a new set of working drawings involving and to do the massive number of recalculations needed. These would require the services of a drawing office with draftsmen and attendant engineers. At best he would have made notations on an existing set of drawings as to the changes to be made.

However, one must ask: given that *Empire Liberty* must have been laid down around the time he was in America and the drawings, specifications and all the necessary calculations would have been prepared many months beforehand, why didn't he simply cable for a set to be sent over to America? Why try and alter existing documentation so that someone else can re-interpret what he wanted done and then prepare new documentation? That doesn't make sense. The only reasonable explanation is that he already had the *Empire Liberty* set with him and it was to that set of documents that he was making relatively small amendments.

Irrespective of how it happened, that *Empire Liberty* formed the next link in the evolutionary chain, *Embassage, Dorington Court, Empire Wind/Empire Wave* is put beyond doubt by Thompson's own in-house history. In 1946 Thompson's produced a 26-page book, *One-Hundred Years Of Shipbuilding 1846-1946*. Tellingly, on page 20, they state:

In 1940, Mr. Robert Cyril Thompson, Managing Director of the firm, and son of the Chairman, Major Robert Norman Thompson, was invited by the Admiralty to proceed to the United States of America as head of the Admiralty Merchant Shipbuilding Mission. The object of the mission was to obtain delivery of about 60 Tramp Cargo Vessels of about 10,000 tons deadweight capacity from the US Shipyards, and also to place contracts with existing Shipyards in Canada. *The parent British vessel from which the American ships were evolved was the EMPIRE LIBERTY* [my emphasis], built at North Sands. The ship was adapted to suit US Production, and it was decided that the ships would be mainly welded . . . *The EMPIRE LIBERTY can be justly claimed as the forebear of the whole fleet of 2710 LIBERTY vessels* [my emphasis] built by the US Government between 1942 and 1945.

I am prepared to accept that as primary evidence as to the progenitor of the 'Ocean' class.

On 1 December news was received that the necessary approval had been given for two new shipyards each to build thirty ships and five days later Thompson boarded the liner *Western Prince* in New York with the necessary contract documents. On 14 December 1940 the liner was torpedoed by the German submarine *U-96* and sunk 400 miles west of the Orkneys. After nine hours in below-freezing conditions, Thompson was one of the lucky 154 persons saved from a total of 169. Despite the dire circumstances, he had the forethought to bring his briefcase with

him and although the contents were sodden and some made unreadable, he was able to have them retyped before making for the Admiralty. Despite the fact that the contract sum was well beyond what had been expected, despite the Chancellor of the Exchequer's protestations, on 20 December contracts were signed with Kaiser-Todd-Bath consortium. One yard was to be built at Richmond, California as Todd-California Shipbuilding Corporation (with Kaiser having a 65 per cent interest) and the other at Portland, Main as Todd-Bath Iron Shipbuilding Corporation with 35 per cent each to Todd and Kaiser and the remaining 30 per cent to Bath Iron works.

With the deal in place, the first sod could be turned to get the massive undertaking started and this is where Kaiser's can-do attitude and experience came to the fore. The Richmond site had been chosen for its access to San Francisco Bay (being directly south of Cutting Boulevard and almost opposite and north of the Golden Gate Bridge). The presence of a Ford Motor Company assembly plant, a Standard Oil refinery, a railway workshop and other small industries in the immediate area with about 23,600 residents and the fact that it was served by the nearby Richmond-San Rafael Car and Passenger Ferry connecting Richmond to Marin County on the opposite shore were contributing factors which must have mitigated the negative aspects presented by the site's topography being far from ideal intertidal marshland. This required that the initial building site of some 100 acres was supported on a grid of some 25,000 concrete piles. These had to be pre-cast, allowed to fully set over twenty-eight days, brought out to the piling rig, lifted into a vertical position and driven into the soft ground. The rig would then have to be moved to the next location – not an easy job in its own right – and the process repeated over and over. Eventually seven self-contained slipways were constructed spanning the three-quarters of a mile of frontage, each backed by its own pre-assembly area. The first keel plates were laid on 14 April 1941 – less than four months after the contracts were signed. Henry J Kaiser certainly had justified the faith the Mission had placed in him.

The Portland, Maine site was like chalk is to cheese compared with Richmond. Where San Francisco Bay was an estuary with a small tidal range, Casco Bay was surrounded by rock with a large tidal range. What was quickly decided upon was to use the tidal range and build three shallow dry docks holding a total of seven ships. This meant blasting the rock behind a temporary cofferdam. Despite these difficulties, this shipyard, again with the same pre-assembly areas complete with cranes was up and running in time for the first keel plates to be laid on 24 May. This was only six weeks later than Richmond's own remarkable achievement but, considering the site difficulties presented by having to excavate in rock and build what were, in effect, three

dry docks, this was a no less noteworthy achievement particularly considering that construction took place during the winter period with heavy frosts.

Just where the 'Ocean'-class name originated is somewhat obscure. What is known is that the policy of naming all ships commandeered by the MOWT with an 'Empire' prefix was thought unsuitable considering where the ships were being built and the anti-imperialist attitude of Americans. Some other prefix was needed, as was the case with the Canadian-built ships (see

Ocean Vanguard, the first of the sixty 'Ocean' class, being launched on 16 August 1941.

Ocean Vanguard undergoing trials, probably in late 1941. Note there is no forecastle. (uboat.net)

Henry J Kaiser with his wife Bess and an early model of a Liberty ship. Note the radial arm davits which were replaced by Welin types. (Saltwater People Historical Society)

tank tests had been encouraging. Quite how a ship with a LOA 501ft 6in, a beam of 68ft 0in and a draft of 29ft 8½in at 15,850 DWT was going to meet the general requirements that had been tentatively decided upon of a LWL of 420ft 0in, LBP of 415ft 0in, beam of 58ft 0in, draft of 26ft 3in and 10,000 DWT is a mystery. You simply cannot scale ship drawings up or down to get a bigger or smaller ship. Naval architecture – like building architecture – simply does not work that way.

A meeting on 8 January with W F Gibbs present plus USMC representatives plus unspecified shipbuilding company representatives – although Todd and Newport News were certainly represented – considered alternatives. Whether one of these was the 'Los Angeles' class is unknown. It would seem unlikely. Perhaps that had been dismissed. In the intervening days, the design of the USMC's yet-to-be-built T2 tanker as an in-principle basis for a new design was explored and this appears to have been put forward. The other was the British design. No decision was reached beyond a common understanding that the emphasis on the emergency ship was to be on standardisation and to enable quick construction by way of minimising the need for furnacing and rolled plating. There seems to have been certain misgivings about the British design due to lack of confirmatory evidence in support of its guiding principles. Gibbs appears to have been the lone voice pointing out, quite correctly I believe, the simple fact that any new ship design – no matter where the design originated – was going to cause delays in the design and testing and documenting process that would be more than offset by any saving in construction time.

By 13 January it seemed that the T2-based design and the British design were on level pegging when it came to the degree of rolled plates required and the complications resulting therefrom. Sometime between 13 January and 7 February a decision was made by the USMC – initially by Admiral Vickery, then it seems backed by Admiral Land – in favour of the British design and Gibbs & Cox were appointed on a 2½-year contract accordingly. According to Bourneuf the first contract was let on 14 March.[9] That's only five weeks after Gibbs & Cox were appointed. It simply beggars belief that Gibbs & Cox could have 'designed' the Liberty ship – and

documented it to sufficient degree to enter into meaningful legal contracts – in so short a time.

To my mind, having earned a large part of my life's income as a professional designer, the term 'design' means to have started with a blank sheet of paper, to have originated, to have conceived, to have thought up, invented, been responsible for, to have created. On the other hand, could Gibbs & Cox have *adapted* an existing design and documented it in that time? Yes, that's just possible, given enough staff and the exigencies of the time. Bear in mind, however, the number of drawings that are required *after* the decisions are made as to what modifications are to be made, how they are to be made, how one modification affects another, what calculations are required, which have to be done again – and the flow-on effect is staggering. I know from experience that these things do not flow smoothly. One unresolved problem can hold up a process which delays another and another. Until the issue is resolved, the bottleneck remains. A whole series of drawings can remain partly in ink, partly in pencil only, waiting for issues to be sorted before they can be fully inked-in, checked over and then sent off for prints to be made. Remember, this was in the day before CAD, indeed before ROtring Rapidograph type pens, when Graphos-type bow-pens where the only permanent drafting medium – slow, cumbersome, difficult and messy to use – before lettering stencils, dry lettering and the like. Drafting linen had to be used before today's more stable and versatile drafting film and the process of making blueprints was slow compared with today's laser printers.

There was nothing ingenious, revolutionary, state-of-the art or cutting edge about the 'design' of the Liberty ship. It was not in any sense a breakthrough in naval architecture. It was very much a bread-and-butter job for the technicians – the naval architects, the engineers, the draftsmen – to adapt something that was tangible, already in existence and proven to meet a relatively simple and uncomplicated design brief. Compared with the ships that Gibbs & Cox had designed from scratch, it was a simple assignment for an experienced and competent office like theirs to produce the basic drawings for the Liberty ship, albeit a much larger one to magnify these into the myriad of super-detailed documents – drawings and specifications – necessary to ensure uniformity of construction and procedures for as trouble-free a production run as possible.

However, what was ingenious about the Liberty ship, and the thing that set it apart from what had come before it and made it a cutting edge in marine construction, was the application of the techniques of prefabrication taken to never-before-seen extents due mainly to the involvement of that extraordinary man, Henry J Kaiser. Traditional shipbuilding was sequential in nature – building, quite literally, from the ground (the keel) upwards. By prefabricating whole sections simultaneously – or, indeed, with some components completed ahead of their requirement – the only limiting factor was the ability to lift or manoeuvre the components into position, and cranes and other devices were designed to overcome this very problem. The result was the remarkable times taken to produce Liberty ships. While man-hour-intensive, these incredible feats were not a function of any inherent ingenuity in the Gibbs & Cox implementation or adaptation of the 'Ocean'-class basics but the prefabrication techniques applied to those basics. It is to Gibbs & Cox's credit that – in an age before computer-aided design – they were able to so successfully document the project in order for those very many

The first keel was laid on 30 April 1941. Now, that's six weeks after contract signing and a reasonable time to allow for start-up. It's feasible that, at the time contracts were signed, all the shop drawings might not have been available, that there was a progressive issuing of these as and when they became available and that the form of contract either allowed a certain amount of 'give and take' (unlikely) or there were provisions in the contracts for these sorts of uncertainties by way of contingencies or Prime Cost items. Even adding this six weeks to the previous five, eleven weeks is an extraordinarily short time to have 'designed' a Liberty ship. It could be considered a good achievement to have adapted the British 'Ocean'-class design to a fully worked-out set of

drawings and attendant specifications, with all the bugs sorted out ready for construction in that eleven weeks.

In keeping with the merchant shipbuilding programme, the new emergency ship was given its own designation: EC-2-SC1. E stood for Emergency, C stood for cargo, as in the existing programme. The 2 represented the fact that it fitted the previously designated 400–450ft length class and the S stood for Steam while C1 related to its design number.

Gibbs & Cox fell out with the USMC in June 1941 when the Commission took over their ordering and purchasing role from the third batch of Liberty ships onwards – 312 having been involved in the first two batches (or waves as they were referred to). By July–August they were finishing the last of the documentation for the sixty 'Ocean' class and the first 312 of the Liberty ships.

> The Commission's staff discovered to its surprise that the plans for the British had not been previously prepared but that the plans for both the British and the Commission's account were being produced simultaneously *and for all practical purposes were the same plans* [my emphasis]. Since it was really all one job, and since the British were paying $600,000 on it, the Commission decided that $500,000 would be more than enough, and on 25 April 1941 made a firm offer on that amount.[10]

The agreed fee had been $750,000 for the first 200 – $3,750 per ship. The USMC increased the first order to 312 ships and expected the fee to remain frozen – reducing the fee-per-ship to $2,404. Gibbs held out for $3,077 per ship – $960,000 but settled on 24 June on the USMC's terms.[11] It was a swings-and-roundabouts equation. Whatever he figured they lost on that contract, they more than made up on the many other USN contracts.

Chapter 14: The Essence of the Liberty Ship

So, what were the significant changes?

- Oil firing in place of coal. This meant deleting the bulkhead at Frame 81 that created the coal bunker and the size of Hold No 3 increased accordingly. Fixed ballast in the double bottom was removed and used for oil bunkers. This required oil filling facilities, extinguishing apparatus and various distribution piping, valves etc – quite a lot of complex plumbing but not, as they now say, rocket science.
- Water-tube boilers in place of Scotch boilers. The boilers were to be of the cross drum, straight tube type fitted with over-deck superheaters based on a Babcock & Wilcox design. These operated at 220 psi and 450°F (232°C) consuming about 30 tons of bunker oil per day at the hull's economic speed of 11 knots. The boilers were, in effect, off-the shelf items but their installation and connections had to be worked out and documented. Again, not rocket science.
- Combining the previously divided accommodation into *one centralised, midships bridge structure* of three levels plus flying bridge. This was not a new or revolutionary idea. Refer, for example, to the British emergency war-built ships of the Type PF [B] and PF [C] which were of similar dimensions to the Liberty ship (448ft 0in LOA, 56ft 0in beam and 7,000–7,300 GRT) and which used the same basic hull and machinery but which had different superstructures, hold and cargo-handling arrangements to suit specific load requirements (see Chapter 6). Note how similar the two drawings are to the 'Ocean' class and the Liberty ship EC2-S-C1, respectively. One consequence of midships superstructure was that engineering and deck staff who had previously been well separated were still deliberately separated within the new bridge structure to suit British sensitivities. Lane says that the midships accommodation was more practical for North Atlantic crossings than the split accommodation and in addition to the

safety offered was more economical with regard to piping and heating.
- Replacement of permanent and removable chain railing to the weather deck by steel bulwarks. This was a simple matter of continuing the frames up to bulwark height, extending the plating and installing scuppers as required.
- All-steel bulwarks to the bridge in place of canvas dodgers. The structure was already there, it was just a matter of infilling it with sheet steel.
- Replacement of round bar/radial davits with Welin-type davits. (Curiously, the 'Ocean' class were fitted with quadrantal davits but Liberty ships retained the simpler Welin type.)
- Reduction from seventy-five different thickness of plating to only twenty-seven. I have no details as to the effect on displacement.
- Reduction in the specified scantlings which saved 430 tons DWT.
- Minimisation or removal of deck camber where possible. Deck camber was simplified by flat runs rather than curved slopes.
- The removal of the tonnage opening at Hatch No 5 that had previously allowed the classification as a shelter-deck type cargo ship.

There may have been 6in of tumblehome in the 'Ocean' class. This was certainly removed.

Minor changes included such things as, *inter alia*: reducing the amount of anchor chain, eliminating the bower anchor, eliminating timber wherever possible save hatch covers which would float in the event of sinking, eliminating the emergency generator, eliminating mechanical ventilation wherever possible, elimination of a fire detection system, no gyrocompass or radio direction finder. The hospital was reduced in size as were crew

LIBERTY SHIP EC2-S-C-1

| No.5 T'ween Decks | No.4 T'ween Decks | No.3 T'ween Decks | No.2 T'ween Decks | No.1 T'ween Decks |

| No.5 Hold | No.4 Hold | No.3 Hold | No.2 Hold | No.1 Hold |

METRES 0   5   10   15   20   25   30

FEET 0   10   20   30   40   50   75   100

lockers and cabins and the finishes in sanitary and galley spaces. While these and many others not mentioned here were largely money-saving, they all had a bearing on whether existing documentation could be used or had to be redrawn.

One major saving was accomplished in the area of the preparation of the critical patterns for the various frames. The process by which these are made involves tables of 'offsets' taken from the hull lines plan and converted in the mould loft into 1:1 templates where they are 'faired'. A parent set was provided from Britain and changed only slightly at bow and stern. Copies were then made available to all builders. Once again, the presence of this sort of information allowed Gibbs & Cox to 'hit the ground running' whereas if they have had to truly design a ship, they would have needed to go through this process from scratch, starting with creating the hull lines – a significant task to begin with – perhaps requiring many revisions before finalisation and many models made for tank testing. This was the very process that the T2 tanker was part way through when under consideration as referred to earlier.

An improvement made to the Liberty ship was the provision of greater ballasting facilities. When the 'Ocean'-class ships were in light condition – such as a Britain to USA convoy – there could be insufficient ballast forward to hold the ship's head down making them becoming difficult to manage. This was not necessarily an issue in a peacetime situation but travelling in convoy with ships two cables one behind the other and three cables apart in rows, this could make station-keeping even more difficult than it already was. In certain conditions, the wind could catch the bow, riding high, like a sail and cause the ship to slew off course. Providing a larger forepeak salt water ballast tank and two deep tanks below Hold No 1 held the bow down lower and provided more and better ballasting alternatives (see Appendix E for specifications)

But, what wasn't changed that could have been? If we come back to the issue of furnacing, lessons could have been learnt from the British from the First World War N class or National Type (see Chapter 2) or what was currently being done with their own emergency shipping (see Chapter 6) with regard to simplifying structure and, particularly, plating by the use of transom sterns – something that has become common place in ship design and construction since in place of the complex curves required by cruiser or counter type sterns. Apparently, nobody thought of this sort of modification to simplify prefabrication and production. It was not as if these N-class ships had been a failure. There were many still serving, sailing in Second World War convoys, ugly maybe, but perfectly seaworthy. The concept could have been readily adapted, especially for a one-way or 'five-year' vessel. It was just easier to re-cycle the 'Ocean'-class hull drawings without significant amendment.

METHODS OF CONSTRUCTION

There are some that argue that the way that the Liberty ships were produced was not mass-production in the sense that motor vehicles are mass-produced on an assembly line – that is, being built up progressively until the vehicle emerges at the end as a complete, ready-to-run unit – but I think it is splitting hairs to say that by building a ship in the one, fixed place and bringing components to it to be fixed in place is not mass-production. The end result is the same. The methodology is, basically, the same.

The ship 'starts' by laying a pre-made keel component into place – the official keel-laying time and date. To this, other major components, such as frames and bulkheads, are added having been prefabricated on-site so that the ship is built up to the point where major sub-assemblies can be added – also either made on-site or constructed off-site and transported to the site. Whole bow and stern sections were made complete as were the main and aft superstructures, their size limited only by the lifting capacity of the cranes. The benefit of this form of construction is that non-skilled labour can be used to do a narrow range of repetitive work on these sub-assemblies so that they are virtually complete when ready to be installed. While this method is very labour intensive and basically cost-inefficient, it can, and did, produce ships in remarkably short times. One should not be dazzled by the four days and 15½ hours taken to build *Robert E Peary*. As a public-relations stunt this was probably incalculable and will always be one of the most remembered 'facts' of the Liberty ships. However, it would be interesting to have actually surveyed that

LIBERTY SHIP WITH BRITISH N-TYPE HULL CONSTRUCTION

A Liberty ship as it may have appeared had the prefabricated type of hull used in the First World War British N class been adopted.

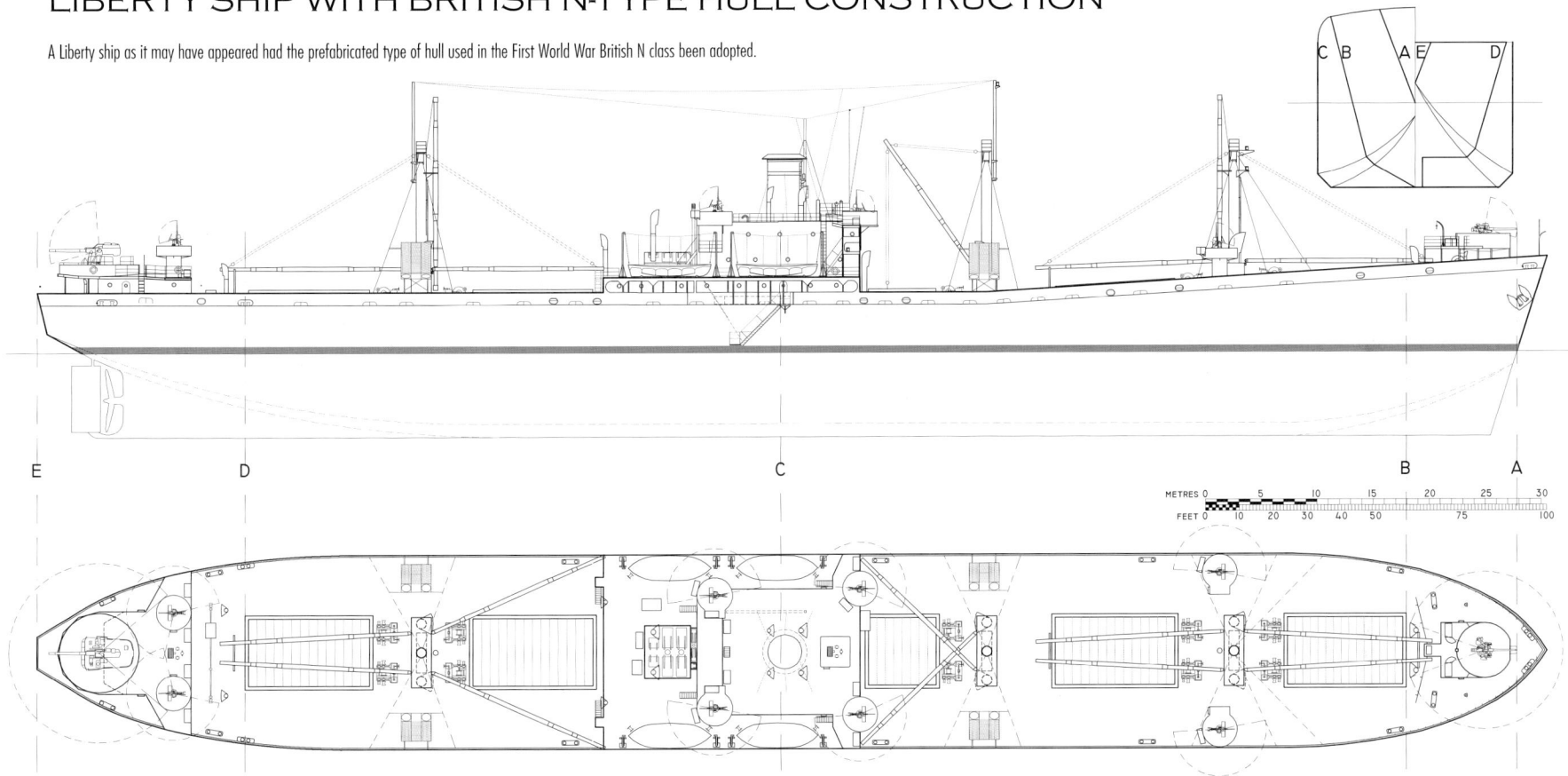

ship after launching and to have viewed the outstanding works and defects list. Ask yourself: how would it be possible to get three coats of enamel-type paint sprayed, rolled or brushed on and dry in that time?

While the method of construction might have been inefficient, what was extremely cost-efficient was the standardisation of fittings and the spreading throughout America of the manufacture of those fittings – all made practical by an extensive and efficient railway network. Contracts could be let

to companies that specialised in a particular type of fitting whether it be large and complex like a deck winch or small and simple like a pipe flange. Either way, the demands of the building programme were met adequately by a flow of parts to the shipyards for all around the country that allowed 2,710 Liberty ships to be built (this number can be disputed) to the point where three ships were being completed each day (on average) in 1943.

Only some Liberty ships were fully welded – those built by the Delta Shipbuilding Co. in New Orleans. Others were mostly

plant's, thus simplifying repairs and maintenance. The same engines were used in the 353 'Fort', 'Park' and 'Victory' ships and the very many similar emergency ships built in Britain. One estimate places the total number of engines made in North America at 3,259 of which the California plant of Joshua Hendy Ironworks were responsible for almost 754.[3] The choice of these engines was also important in that it accessed a pool of experienced seagoing engineering personnel familiar with the type, its operation and its maintenance.

In the most basic of terms, the engine was a vertical, inverted, direct-acting, condensing, three-cylinder, triple-expansion type having a high-pressure cylinder of 24.5in diameter, a medium-pressure cylinder of 37in diameter and a low-pressure cylinder of 70in diameter all operating at a stroke of 48in, all being fed by steam at a pressure of 220 psi (pounds per square inch) at a maximum (superheat) temperature of 450°F (232°C) with 26in of vacuum. It produced 2,500 IHP (indicated horsepower) at 76 RPM (revolutions per minute) driving a four-bladed propeller of 18ft 6in diameter giving a hull speed of 11 knots.

The boilers providing the essential steam were no less 'old fashioned', having been of a type first built in 1899 based on a Babcock and Wilcox design but modified for oil-firing and were used extensively since the First World War. They were simple, reliable and easily fabricated. Technically, they were of the cross-drum, sectional sinuous header, straight-tube design with superheaters. The boilers were generally reliable given the wide variety of fuels available and the often-limited turnaround times for necessary maintenance.

THE NAME LIBERTY SHIP

There has always been controversy about where and from whom the Liberty ship name originated. There's nothing particularly spiritually uplifting in referring to the EC2 ships. Worse, using the terms 'Emergency' from the first letter of the EC2 designation had negative connotations.

The public-relations experts latched on to the American War of Independence hero Patrick Henry's closing words at his address at St. John's Church, Richmond, Virginia on 23 March 1775: 'Give me liberty, or give me death!' However, when did this actually happen?

The *Patrick Henry* was, quite appropriately from a PR point of view, the very first Liberty ship launched – on 27 September 1941. This was called 'Liberty Fleet Day' and fourteen emergency ships were launched at various shipyards around America including one 'Ocean' class (*Ocean Voice*).

Elphick quotes a Postscript in a letter from Thompson's to the Admiralty on 19 July 1941 relating to Hull No 611: 'In view of the fact that this vessel is the *parent type for those building in Canada and the USA* [my emphasis and these words are important in themselves] we think that special consideration be given to its name. As ships building in America are known as the Liberty fleet we suggest that an appropriate name would be *Empire Liberty*'.[4] He claims that this letter confirms that the use of the name Liberty ship was common in Britain and that this letter 'clears the matter up conclusively'. What may have been promoted one side of the Atlantic was not necessarily known or accepted the other side.

However, written evidence of the use of the term 'Liberty ship' comes much earlier – 8 November 1940 – in the form of Admiral Land's files. There is a Memorandum from Land to Mr Knudsen (presumably W S Knudsen, Chairman of the Office of Production Management) and in the top right-hand corner appear the words '**Liberty – Design**'.[5] Similarly, on 18 November a Memorandum on the subject of Prefabricated Ships has the same 'Liberty – Design' heading in the top right-hand corner,[6] and on 26 December 1940, a very critical Memorandum for the President: Summary – Project 200 Merchant Marine Ships, has that very same heading.[7] So, unless someone can find a source earlier than 8 November 1940, I credit Admiral E S Land with being the author of the term Liberty Ship.

THE 'UGLY DUCKLING' SOBRIQUET

President Roosevelt was not impressed with the plans for the emergency cargo ships when he was presented with them in January 1941. Apparently, he termed them 'dreadful looking objects' but it was *Time* magazine that coined the term 'ugly duckling'. With all due respects to President Roosevelt, I doubt if he was experienced enough to be able to make a valued judgement, particularly from a set of architect's plans – and probably only an abbreviated set at that. These are not the easiest things to read unless you are experienced. Lines on drawings can mean nothing or everything, depending on your background, experience and training. To some it can be looking at an Aztec codex and be totally meaningless and confusing. To others, each line, each intersection of lines although seen in one dimension on a sheet of paper can be interpreted three-dimensionally. Personally, I do not think the Liberty ship – or its predecessor – was ugly, especially compared with many of the graceless and strictly functional commercial ships of today. The hull had a reasonable sheer and the balance of the midships structure – while not in itself a particularly elegant or noteworthy statement – sat comfortably slightly aft of midships with two masts forward and one mast aft of it. If there was any discordant feature it was, perhaps, the funnel which, with a bit more thought, could have been blended into the superstructure a little better – as, indeed, did happen with some of the post-war modernisations. But the superstructure had to support anti-aircraft gun positions and provide them with good firing arcs – which it did – as well as accommodate the officers and crew and four 24ft lifeboats.

HULL CRACKS

As with the 'ugly duckling' sobriquet, it is unfortunate that Liberty ships are also remembered by many for the much hyped-up publicity about them breaking in two due to faulty welding. Three were definitely known to have broken in half but there were well over a thousand instances of cracks due to brittle fractures. The type of steel used resulted in it changing character from ductile to brittle in the low temperatures experienced in the North Atlantic. Further, structural design faults created extra stresses around square openings such as deck hatches all made worse by overloading and the stresses imposed by rough seas. Riveted ships to the same design with the same steel did not experience the cracking, hence the blame was placed, unfairly, on welding. The problems were quickly overcome by reinforcement around these sorts of openings which in many ways duplicated what the riveting achieved in the first place.

THE 'SAM' SHIPS

A total of somewhere between 177 and 200 Liberty ships were made available to Britain under the terms of the Lend Lease agreement – more specifically the Defense Aid Supplemental Appropriation Act, 1941. Records as to numbers vary. Sawyer and Mitchell refer to 'some 200' but the index count reveals only 186. Elphick states the number as being 182.[8] Whatever the number, all but one were given 'Sam' prefixes. A common myth was that this was to distinguish them as being from 'Uncle Sam' but it was simply to signify that, contrary to the 'Ocean' class and its derivatives with their split superstructures and a Hold No 3 between bridge and funnel, these ships had a **S**uperstructure **A**mid **S**hip. American largesse was both tried and tired in 1947 when it became obvious that 'SAM' ships were operating at a lower cost than American ships on shipping routes vital to the USA. The immediate remedy sought was recall the SAM ships to American ownership or buy them outright. Sawyer and Mitchell's explanation of how this panned out is a bit confusing.[9] Apparently the British Government had to approve of British shipowners bidding up to £137,000 but they then say, '*All* [my emphasis] the British-flagged Liberties

were then "technically" returned to America, although in practice many were still retained by their operators whilst the legalities of outright purchase were performed. The others were returned to America and many of these were placed into the reserve fleet.'

ARMAMENT

The drawings generally available of Liberty ships are relatively consistent in the armament depicted although not necessarily very detailed as to the armament. From what I have been able to determine, the most basic armament fit for the first ships was:

Bow: 37mm Gun M1[*]
Midships: 2 x 20mm Oerlikons (bridge wings)[**]
Stern: 5in/38 cal possibly Mk 21[***]
            2 x 20mm Oerlikons (raised in gun tubs, port and starboard).

The more usual fit seems to have been:
Bow: 3in/50 cal Mk 20–22
            Midships:4 x 20mm Oerlikons (2 x bridge wings, 2 x aft end of superstructure)
Stern: 5in/38 cal possibly Mk 21 or Mk 37 in some cases.
            2 x 20mm Oerlikons (raised in gun tubs, port and starboard)

[*]   This was a US Army weapon and was soon abandoned.
[**]   The 20mm Oerlikon model type is unknown. Photos show both the most common Mk 2 or 4 mount with their elevating handwheel and also the fixed pedestal Mk 5 Mod 3 or Mk 9–10 with the stepped gunner's platform.
[***] There may have been simpler models. I have seen references to 4in guns being fitted and this seems to have been the 4in/50 cal removed from the 'four-stack' destroyers.

Over time, additional 20mm Oerlikons were added in elevated gun tubs abeam the masts and, in some cases, abeam and slightly aft of the 3in mount.

LIFESAVING EQUIPMENT

I would have liked to been able to detail the various measures taken over time by way of life rafts but was simply unable to unearth any details. Each Liberty ship in standard form had a complement of four 24ft lifeboats. These all seem to have been made by the Globe American Corporation, a small manufacturer of kitchen stoves and heaters that saw an opening and ended up turning out the 24ft steel lifeboats at the rate of one every two hours. Lifeboats cannot always be launched in some conditions, get damaged in action or cannot be reached by all crew members so a range of quick-release life rafts was developed. These were supported on steel frames, located generally close by the masts where they did not interfere with the derricks in such a way that being angled and well above deck, gravity would ensure release even at angles of heel. These rafts seem to vary from rather crude rectangular, timber slatted affairs, basically platforms supported on 55-gallon (US) oil drums – at least to begin with – and ended up as almost boat-shaped rafts more akin to Carley floats in appearance in that they were, or appeared to be, compartmentalised, rectangular tubular construction with some sort of floor – either watertight like a boat (which seems unlikely given that they were jettisoned and would be subject to damage) or slatted like a Carley float, and with thwarts which were floats in themselves. Canadian-built equivalents – the 'Forts' and 'Victories' and the like – seem to have been equipped at some late stage with double-ended, canoe-shaped equivalents. In desperation, I even searched the various modelmakers' accessories for clues as to types, sizes and construction of the many life rafts only to find a similar lack of uniformity.

The most primitive version of the life rafts. (ssarkansan.org)

A more advanced type of life raft but still makeshift in nature. (ssarkansan.org)

The first purpose-designed and manufactured life raft.

This Canadian version is almost a lifeboat in design.

Fort Chilcotin. Note the similarity of the sheer to that of the Liberty ship and a slight rake to the funnel apparent. (City of Vancouver Archives, CVA 195-2)

of the more familiar air-cooled American M2 HB (Heavy Barrel). I very much doubt that they were the Vickers .50 – indeed I hope not as these were an inferior weapon. The Browning M2 – the 'Ma Deuce' – is still in use today. The Browning may have been fitted before Oerlikons became available or were fitted in the bridge wings when Oerlikons were available but in insufficient numbers or were used to augment a full or partial Oerlikon fit-out. Another possibility is that, being a lighter mounting than the Oerlikon, they were more easily accommodated in the bridge wings. In addition, there were probably PAC rockets and other such useless make-do contraptions designed to bring down aircraft by ensnaring them in cables sent aloft by rockets.

The 'Pillar Box' was found to be ineffective and was replaced by Oerlikons or, perhaps, by 40mm Bofors. While the 12-pounder was an old gun it was very reliable, capable of a good rate of fire and quite effective as an anti-aircraft weapon. Conversely, the 4in QF Mk XIX was nicknamed the 'Woolworths Gun' as a reflection of the type and price of goods then sold by that chain. It was a low-velocity weapon and, while used on corvettes and frigates, was little regarded: 'A feeble weapon of misguided conception . . . which was mistakenly expected to make a bang loud enough to sustain morale of the merchant seaman whilst at a ridiculously short range, produce a splash big enough to make the submarine dive' (Commander H Stokes-Rees, RN, 1948).

CHAPTER 16: THE ROYAL NAVY'S MAINTENANCE SHIPS

As an amateur historian, one thing that has always amazed me when studying the Second World War is the confidence the Allies had that they were always going to win the conflict – despite many setbacks – and, particularly, the considerable forward planning that took place on that basic assumption.

One example is the establishment of the British Pacific Fleet (BPF). Its predecessor, the British Eastern Fleet, had been based in Ceylon and operated, essentially, in the Indian Ocean. The BPF was based – to begin with – in Sydney but moved to Manus Island, New Guinea. While it was not officially formed until 22 November 1944, it took many months to assemble. A feature of the fleet was the fleet train – the support vessels needed to supply a highly mobile fleet operating over great distances without access to ports. One such vessel was a maintenance or repair ship capable of effecting all manner of at-sea repairs from battle damage to regular maintenance of electrical, mechanical and hydraulic equipment.

Sixteen of the Canadian-built 'Victory'-class ships were commissioned into the Royal Navy – starting in early 1945 – as maintenance ships of five different types: Escort Maintenance, Armament Maintenance, Coastal Craft Maintenance, Landing Craft Maintenance, Landing Ship Tank Maintenance. The end of the war saw most of these ships redundant and some were placed in reserve. Five of the original twenty-one ordered were completed as merchant ships.

The Escort Maintenance Ship HMS *Hartland Point* somewhere in the Far East judging by the crew's tropical rig. (shipsnostalgia.com)

HMS *ASSISTANCE*

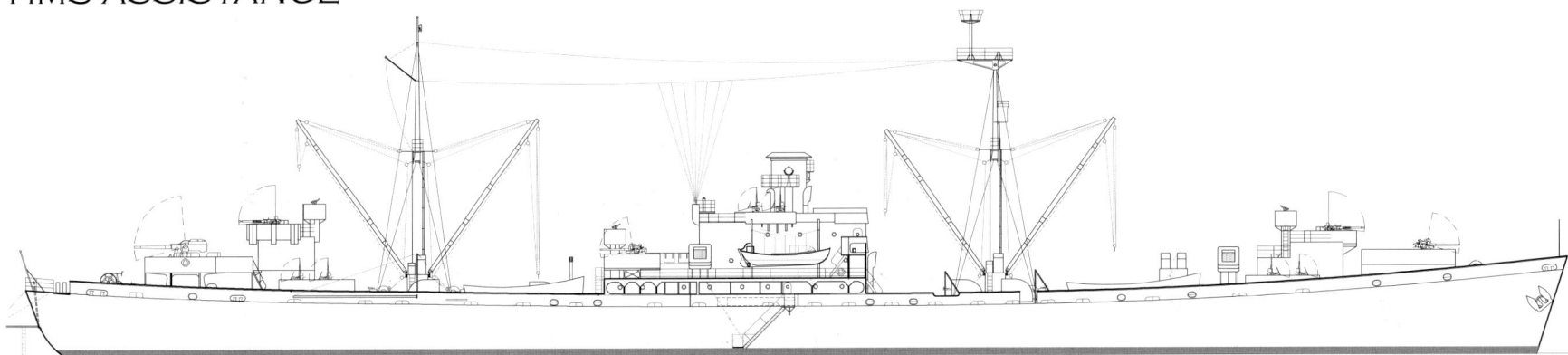

HMS *Assistance* and her sister-ship HMS *Diligence* were ordered in the United States as repair ships of the USN's *Xanthus* class and were expected to serve in the British Pacific Fleet. Their armament was a 5in/38 cal Mk 21 or 37, three 3in/50 cal Mk 22, four 40mm Bofors and no less than twelve 20mm Oerlikons, attesting to the threat posed by Japanese aircraft in the Pacific theatre.

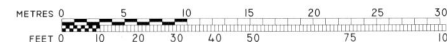

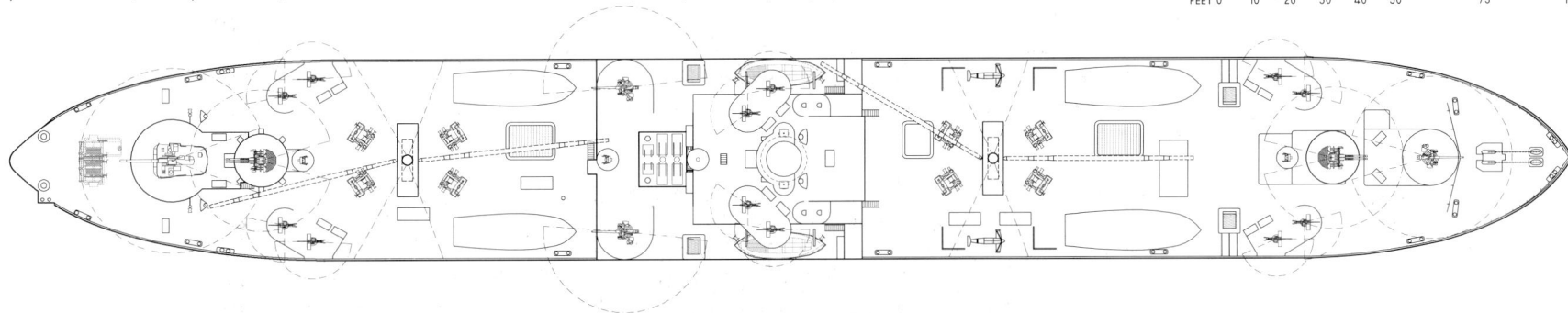

generation from 3 x 20KW to 3 x 50KW turbo generators, had four extra winches and condensate pumps accordingly plus minor items to accommodate additional personnel. The original number planned was twenty-seven but this was reduced to eight as specialised Landing Ships Tank (LST) came off the slips.

USS *Laertes*, a repair ship converted from a Liberty ship, late in the Second World War . (Naval History & Heritage Command NH 107749)

REPAIR SHIPS (ARG)

The highly mobile nature of the Pacific campaign – and to some extent the amphibious operations in North Africa and the Mediterranean – resulted in the need for repair and maintenance facilities that could follow and service the fleet's needs. While specific depot ships had existed for submarines and destroyers and the navies had dedicated repair ships between the two wars, the growing technicality meant that ships were needed to deal with electronics, with internal combustion engines, with armaments of widely varied types and sizes. The EC2 hull was

ARMY AIRCRAFT REPAIR SHIP – ARU

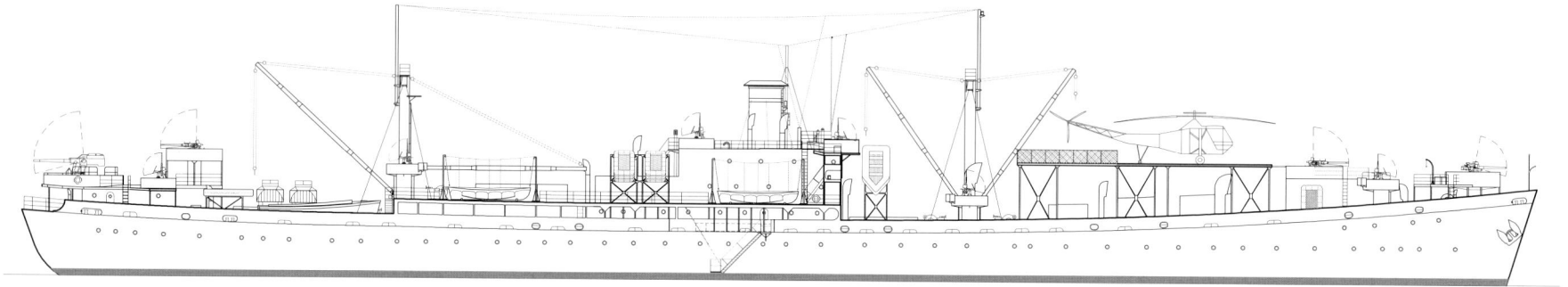

The United States Army and Army Air Force operated their own fleet of ships, amongst which were ships especially to take care of aircraft repairs in forward areas. In this case a helicopter, one of the earliest operational in wartime conditions, is housed on a raised flight-deck and was used to transfer material and personnel. Armament: 1 x 5in/38 cal Mk 21 or Mk 37, 1 x 3in/50 cal Mk 22, 2 x 40mm Bofors, 12 x 20mm Oerlikons.

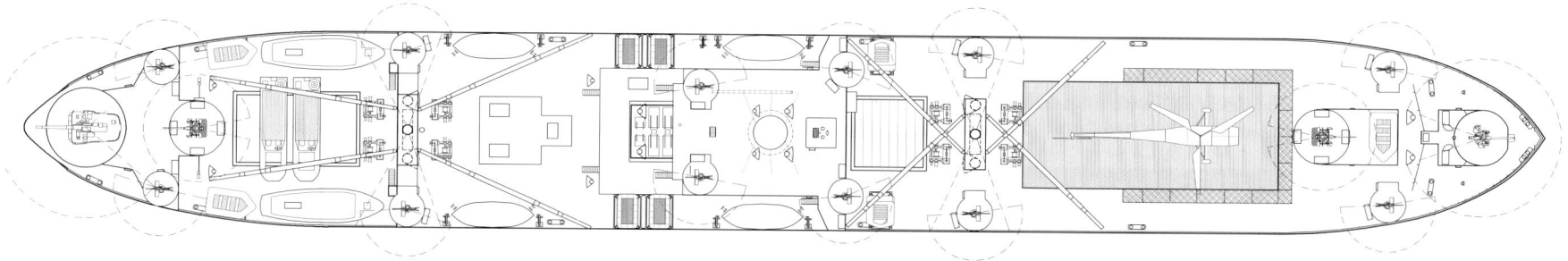

from Houston, Texas to Cristobal in the Canal Zone. Four hulls under construction were designated and plans drawn up by Gibbs & Cox to enable loads of 10,000 tons but this load required that fuel could only be carried for a one-way voyage. The plans were dropped in June 1942 and the hulls were completed as normal EC2s.

SURVEILLANCE SHIPS

The Cold War gave rise to the Distant Early Warning (DEW) Line– a chain of radar stations in the northern Arctic region of

Who could pick USAHS *Dogwood* as having a Liberty ship hull? (photoship.co.uk)

ARMY HOSPITAL SHIP

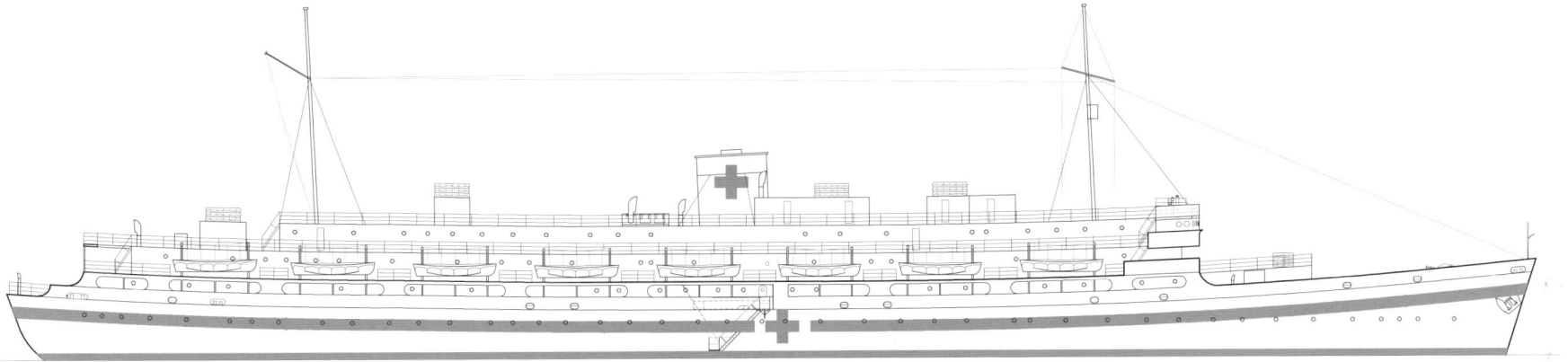

The United States Army Hospital Ships that were converted from basic Liberty ship hulls were used to transport patients rather than treat casualties.

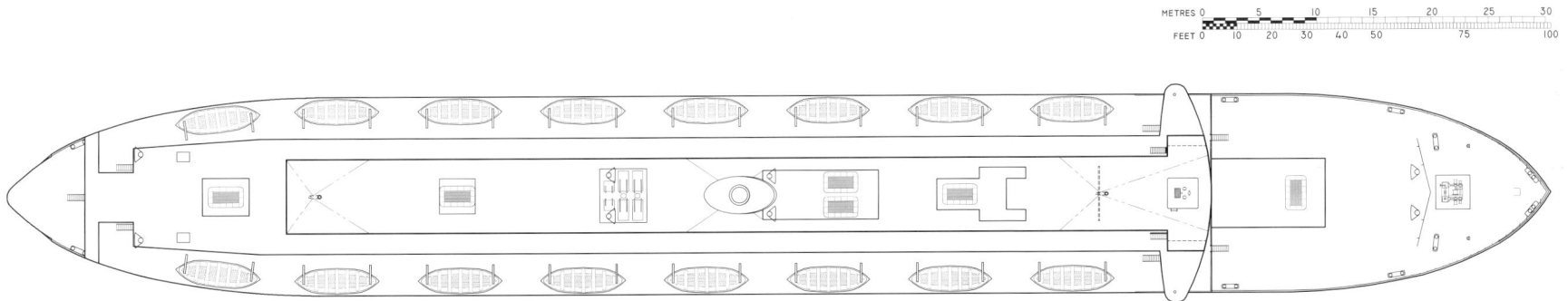

METRES 0 ... 5 ... 10 ... 15 ... 20 ... 25 ... 30
FEET 0 ... 10 ... 20 ... 30 ... 40 ... 50 ... 75 ... 100

Canada augmented by additional stations along the north coast, the Aleutian Islands, the Faroe Islands, Greenland and Iceland. Its sole purpose was to detect the intrusion of Soviet aircraft or a nuclear strike. The DEW Line was supplemented by two 'barrier' forces in the Atlantic and Pacific Oceans. These consisted of surface picket stations plus two surface naval forces. One was of twelve radar picket destroyer escorts and the other sixteen *Guardian*-class radar picket ships – conversions of Z-EC2-S-C5 boxed aircraft transports. It is not known why this particular version was chosen. An air wing of Lockheed WV-2 Warning Star aircraft further extended the picket lines.

The picket ships (*Guardian* class designated YAGR then AGR) operated from 1955 to 1965 – eight on the East Coast and eight on the West Coast. They had a crew of 13 officers, 8 chief petty officers, and 125 enlisted men and were on station for 30–45 days at a time, about 400–500 miles offshore in a specific zone. Their only armament was two token 3in/50 cal single mounts – one bow and one stern. They had a very extensive radar outfit which

The impressive array of high-tech antennae on the low-tech twenty-year-old ex-Liberty ship. (navsource.org)

Unfortunately, there are few photographs of USAS *American Mariner* in her role as a missile-tracking ship and this poor reproduction is the most comprehensive view. (navsource.org)

OTHER CONVERSIONS

Liberty ships were not only easily adaptable and plentiful, but also considered expendable. In 1957, at least one, and possibly three were taken from reserve and converted into experimental minesweepers. The propelling machinery was removed and the hull was filled with empty oil drums. For propulsion, four T-34 steerable turbo-prop (total 24,000 HP) engines were installed – two at the bow and two at the stern and apparently gave a speed of 8 knots. The intention, according to navsource.org, was to 'bump into mines and blast a path through a minefield'. The only one for which I could find a photograph was the *John L Sullivan*, named after the heavyweight boxer, the Great John L or the Boston Strong Boy.

Another unusual conversion was the uss *American Mariner* which had begun its career as a cadet training ship. This conversion involved an appearance somewhat along the lines of the hospital ship conversion but not extending as far forward or aft and with the boat deck one deck higher. She was reactivated as a missile range instrumentation ship in 1957 with an array of large radar and tracking antennae added. In 1959 she was transferred to the US Army and assigned to Advanced Research Guided Missiles Agency as US Army Ship *American Mariner* but manned by civilians and remained as a missile tracking ship until 1 January 1964 when she was assigned to the Atlantic Missile Range under USAF and Pan American control then transferred to the USN Military Sea Transportation Service as USNS *American Mariner* (T-AGM-12) finally out of service some time in 1966, ending up as an aerial bombing target.

CHAPTER 21: POPULAR MISCONCEPTIONS

It is frustrating that, having found the basic story – and that was no secret had people bothered to read Peter Elphick's book at the very least – that what I can only refer to as rubbish and hyperbole is still printed and distributed widely on the subject of the Liberty ship.

The Internet is, in many ways, a wonderful thing – both a blessing and a curse. It can be a source of valuable information. It can also be a disturbing spreader of disinformation and plagiarism. One can often find the same sentences repeated verbatim without reference to the original source. So-called 'facts' become accepted truths without question and without explaining their source. Too often simply using a group of key search words can lead to numerous sites where, quite obviously, the same information had been cut and pasted carelessly from some unidentifiable 'original' source that got in wrong in the very first place.

Unfortunately, distortions of the truth due to lack of knowledge if told often enough tend to become accepted as fact.

Here's some that didn't meet the test, and in no particular order:

- From u-s-history.com: 'During World War II, Kaiser became known as "the father of modern shipbuilding." *His Liberty design* [my emphasis] was used for ships built by the United States Maritime Commission.' Kaiser's design? Really?
- From Wikipedia: 'Under the direction of Major Robert Norman Thompson and his son, Robert Cyril Thompson, research *led to the creation of a distinctive new ship model – the Liberty Ship* [my emphasis].'

Some authors who should have done some more research about *Dorington Court*:

- Spencer C. Tucker's book, *World War II at Sea: An Encyclopedia, Volume I* under a heading referring to the

Liberty Ship by Paul E Fontenoy states: 'The British ship, *Dorington Court of 1939 was the basis of the Liberty Ship design* [my emphasis]' adapted for welded construction with improved crew accommodation.'
- Nicholas Veronico's book, *World War II Shipyards by the Bay* states much the same: 'The British were seeking sixty ships, known as the Ocean Class and *based on J. L. Thompson and Sons-designed and built-Dorington Court* [my emphasis]'.
- Guy Span, a publicist for the SS *Jeremiah O'Brien*, one of the two restored Liberty ships, states in 'A Working Ship' that the (Merchant Shipbuilding) Mission 'wanted an order of 60 ugly little freighters . . . *built to plans provided, the specs of the utilitarian tramp freighter, SS Dorington Court* [my emphasis]'. His piece goes on to say, 'However, America was busy, its shipyards gearing up to build a fleet of national defense steam turbine freighters, faster and more efficient than the inelegant British design.' He finishes by saying, 'Thus, on September 27, 1941 the first SS *Dorington Court* vessel was launched, re-classed as a "Liberty" ship and appropriately named the SS *Patrick Henry*. On October 15, 1941, its mate was launched for England, as the first of sixty, the SS *Ocean Vanguard*.' Apart from his pejorative language displaying an Anglophobic bias – did the mission specifically want 'ugly little freighters?' – he displays a remarkable ignorance of the facts, particularly as to *Dorington Court* in two instances. The inelegant, little freighter he derides became the Liberty ship he promotes.

All have made the same mistake of accepting *Dorington Court* as the base. It simply wasn't, because the drawings for that ship had been made redundant by the *Empire Wind* group of ships and the *Empire Liberty* group of ships which Thompson's designed and were building at the time followed, of course, by the 'Ocean' class.

To say that the Liberty ship was based on *Dorington Court* would be akin to saying that the 1937 Model Ford was based on

The tramp ship *Stakesby* built in 1880 by Joseph L Thompson & Sons Lts. Photographed in the Avon River, North Somerset with Isambard Kingdom Brunel's famous Clifton Suspension bridge in the background. (searlecanada.com)

However, just looking at the Gross Registered Tonnages (the Lengths are probably LBPs and not LOAs), the largest – *Crane* or *Sybil* – are a far cry from the sort of tonnage, length and beam to say that the 'Ocean' class or the Liberty designs was based on a British tramp steamer of 1879, or words to that effect. Averaged out, *Crane* and *Sybil* are 28 per cent of a Liberty's GRT, 61.4 per cent of a Liberty's LOA, 59.9 per cent of a Liberty's depth and 64.3 per cent of a Liberty's beam. My drawing opposite is typical of a tramp ship like those built by Thompson's.

Certainly, the opening of the Suez Canal in 1869 stimulated tramp ship evolution, accentuated in the 1880s by the VTE and by steel replacing iron plates. Hurd gives credit to the shipbuilders of the Tyne, Wear and later Hartlepool as being 'pioneers of this immense transformation'.[6] The River Wear was, of course, Thompson's base. Looking at other examples of 'General Cargo' ships built around 1879 in Britain, many were clipper-bowed with short bowsprits, still rigged with auxiliary sails, mostly fore-and-aft gaff-rigged but some still setting square sails on the foremast, all to support their two-cylinder compound engines and reduce coal consumption. Many of the Royal Navy's ships were similarly rigged with auxiliary sails and, of course, windjammers were still being built until the turn of the century.

However, according to Fenton, it wasn't until 1890 that the three-island design principle – that is, forecastle, bridge deck and poop deck separated by well decks having one or more holds – began to grow in popularity.[7] But, what these three-island designs did NOT have that was emblematic of the direct ancestors of the Liberty ship was the split bridge deck with a No 3 hold and coal hold between the bridge and the boiler room and engine room spaces. Fenton says this did not appear until around 1900.[8] However, in appearance, the Hog Islanders (Types A and B) owed more to a three-island ship than the Liberty ship's direct ancestors – but no American author, quick to link the British tramp steamer of the Merchant Shipbuilding Commission of 1940 to a design going back to 1879, ever mentioned that.

It seems to me, as an outsider looking in with no national axe to grind, that the reporting on the Liberty ship has generally been through American eyes and there has been a marked tendency to deliberately minimise the British involvement in its development by near-silence or by acts of omission on the subject or to positively denigrate and belittle that involvement by the deliberate use of language. If it hadn't been for that 'inelegant British design', those 'sixty ugly little freighters', those 'powered scows', 'based on an old 1879 tramp steamer', what would have been the outcome?

For every one of these examples I have quoted above I am sure that, in books, on line, in newspaper articles and the like there are dozens more. Who knows how many school assignments have blandly repeated as gospel the . . . well, let's just be kind and call them, 'inaccuracies'? Hopefully, the evidence presented in this book sets the record straight.

TRAMP SHIP CIRCA 1879

This is a typical example of the type of tramp ship built by Joseph L Thompson & Sons in 1879. Various authors have drawn a dubious connection between this type of vessel and the Liberty ship.

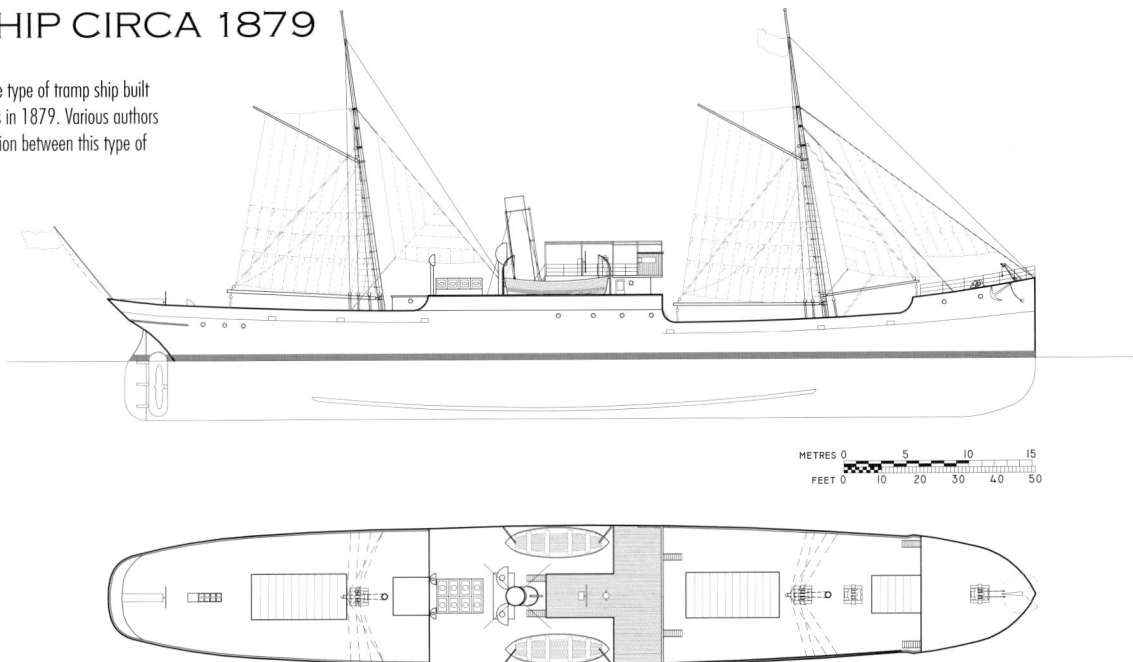

CONCLUSION

That Cyril Thompson was the father of the Liberty ship is a fact that cannot be denied. His company's designs that flowed from *Embassage* through *Dorington Court* to the *Empire Wind* series (Hull No 601–10) to *Empire Liberty* to the 'Ocean' class are undeniable as the heritage of the Liberty ships (see Appendix F). His dynamic leadership of the Merchant Shipbuilding Mission is well documented. Without that leadership, and perhaps without access to the plans that led to the 'Ocean' class, perhaps the building of 'Ocean' class ships would have been delayed at best, or stillborn at worst. The results, either way, can only be imagined. The effects of delays? Problematical. Certainly, difficult to assess. How many less ships making a successful crossing of the Atlantic would have made the difference? Without doubt, no 'Ocean' class would have meant no 'Fort'-type ships and meant no Liberty ships – at least in the format that we know them. That the United States would have produced some sort of substitute – of the five-year, slow, disposable nature of the Liberty ship with reciprocating engines – is unlikely. That simply did not fit the USMC philosophy. The lesson of Hog Island still dogged America. They didn't want a repeat of building too many ships, too late and too unsuited for a peacetime merchant marine. It is likely that they would have pursued their existing policy, despite the problems of the bottlenecks with turbines. However, as with the destroyer escorts, where the American can-do attitude prevailed and answers were found in diesel-electric propulsion, who is to say that C-type ships destined for steam turbines would not have been alternatively powered? But could they have been delivered in sufficient numbers in sufficient time?

More is owed Cyril Thompson than his CBE (Commander of the Most Excellent Order of the British Empire) awarded in June 1941 could ever represent. At around 34 years of age this was no mean feat in itself, there being two classes of award below the CBE – the OBE (the O standing for Order, or

'Other Buggers' Efforts' as often deprecated!) then the MBE – (the M standing for Member, or similarly deprecated to 'Many Buggers' Efforts!'). Elphick suggests that he was offered a knighthood – the second highest award of a KBE (Knight Commander of the Most Excellent Order of the British Empire) – but would not accept it until his father was so honoured and which never happened.[1] However, I looked up Robert Norman Thompson's obituary (*The Times*, Wednesday, 3 October 1951) and note that he was knighted five years later in 1946. The obituary gives no details as to the nature of the award itself. An Internet search of the 1946 awards indicates the award of Knight Bachelor was for 'services to shipbuilding'. Quite why Cyril Thompson thought his father deserved that honour is, therefore, particularly unclear considering the very obvious contribution Cyril Thompson made. Just proof that blood's thicker than water.

Elphick states:

> Cyril was to become one of the unsung heroes behind the Allied victory in the Second World War, arguably THE unsung hero in view of the huge importance of his contribution and the rather less than proportionate recognition he received.[2]

Feeling his work was done he applied to join the Royal Navy, was knocked back on the grounds that his work was too important. In what must seem an out-of-character move that has somewhat weird parallels with the author, T E. Lawrence (*Seven Pillars of Wisdom*), Thompson joined the Royal Air Force as the lowest-ranked Aircraftsman, Second Class – a flight mechanic, a role for which he was, surely, over-qualified. He quickly rose to Flight Sergeant and was commissioned just before the end of the war, after which he re-joined the company and assumed joint control with his brother becoming chairman in 1951 after the death of his father. He died on 10 March 1967.

Elphick states:

> It was the sad and sudden end to the life of a man who among all unsung Allied heroes of the Second World War, probably did more than most to win it. (Appendix G, *Times* Obituary) [3]

I could not have put it better myself.

When I look back at my first notes made when setting out to write this book, I realise what a significant change there was over time in the general direction it took. I hadn't intended any part of the book to be controversial – simply an historical record. But, when I discovered the significance of the work done by that small, out-of-work Sunderland shipyard in the mid-1930s and what the spin-doctored world has come to regard as the all-American Liberty ship, I wanted to put that record straight. Yes, there are references to Thompson's in the various books on the subject – but they are largely passing references, almost begrudgingly in some cases. How could a country as big and powerful as the United States of America possibly have produced 2,710 ships to a design made so simple and so cost-effective by a never-heard-of-shipyard-on-some-little-known-river-in-England? No, that never happened – and that's basically what the world has come to believe. It suited the American psyche. The razzmatazz of 'Liberty Fleet Day' – fourteen emergency ships launched in one day – massaged their undoubted can-do spirit. The Liberty ship and the hype surrounding it fitted comfortably with the American view of the world. It still does to the point where, almost eighty years later, Gibbs and Cox's website claims, proudly that they 'designed the famous, standardized cargo-carrying Liberty ships of World War II'.

If I was to take a yacht designed by that equally famous firm of American naval architects, Sparkman and Stephens, say, for instance their well proven *S & S 34* (1967) which has probably made more solo circumnavigations of the world than any other single class of yacht and design a different deck and cabin top for it – perhaps to give more headroom or a perhaps a pilot house, even alter the rig from masthead sloop to a cutter or a fractional rig and put in a lighter diesel engine relocated aft (as has been done in some *S & S 34s*) – I could not then claim it to be a new yacht and say that I designed it. That would be totally unethical. Sparkman and Stephens had already done the hard work designing the hull, working out the very critical shapes that allow it to perform well on all points of sail at all angles of heel, establishing the correct ballast ratio and placement of that ballast assisted in this case by the location of the engine not under the cockpit as was usual in 1967 but midships where its weight was better distributed. They'd designed the rudder shape to be effective, established the correct balance between the Centre of Effort of the sail plan and the Centre of Lateral Resistance of the hull under different sailing conditions. By putting a different deck on it and a different rig all I would be doing making alterations which particularly suited me. It would still be an *S & S 34* and its distinctive hull shape and its attributes recognisable as such by any experienced yachtsman! No change in cabin top or rig would conceal that basic fact.

How much different is this from what Gibbs and Cox did with the Liberty ship? Sure, they changed the construction from riveted to welded – but that had already been done with the 'Ocean'-class hull. That's not such a big deal, just a lot of redrafting of details. Sure, they changed the boilers. No big deal either – take one set out and put another different set in the same boiler room. That's a bit like taking one engine out of the *S & S 34* and installing some other one. That's not rocket science. Sure, they changed the accommodation – and for the better I might add. No big deal either. A big, three-level box with a hole in the middle for the boiler uptake and accommodation placed around it. Again, nothing out of the ordinary here. Did they design that? Well, yes, they did. No question about it. But, revolutionary? No. Logical, yes, repeating – in basic principle – what had already been done in many previous designs? Absolutely. Indeed, as I stated in Chapter 15, the British emergency war-built ships of the PF [B] and PF [C] type are of similar dimensions to the Liberty ship that used the same basic hull and machinery but which had different superstructures, hold and cargo-handling arrangements to suit specific load requirements.

So, appearance-wise, their stamp on the 'design' was: bulwarks instead of chain railings, two masts forward of the superstructure, the superstructure itself and . . . well, I can't think of anything else. Did they put some rake to the funnel? No. Did they trick the 'design' up in any visual way at all? No. But, like the *S & S 34*, the hull and its hydrodynamics remained the same. The means of propulsion remained the same! Frederick Lane said, in his book, published in 1951 and, as such, the seminal work on the subject:

> The minor changes just enumerated [similar to those in my paragraph, above] did not affect the vessels' appearance. It was the single midship house in place of the fore and aft houses, the different cargo handling equipment [?] and the solid weather-deck bulwarks instead of chain rails that made the Liberty ship look different from the Ocean class vessel . . . The Liberty ship and their British prototypes were sisters under the skin so to speak.[4]

The reason I query the reference to 'different cargo handling equipment' is that I can only think that Lane must be referring to his earlier comment in the book that the Liberty ship had masts replacing kingposts. This is incorrect as the only kingposts in the Ocean Class were those to port and starboard abeam the funnel serving the small Hold No 3 – all other holds were being served by masts identical in appearance and in all practical operating respects to those which were included in the Liberty ship. So, what exactly did Gibbs and Cox actually *design*? Just what was worth the David W. Taylor Gold Medal of the Society of Naval Architects and Marine Engineers? (See Chapter 13.)

Perhaps things are, or were, different in America. Perhaps things were different in the case of the Liberty ship because Thompson's used in-house naval architects. Perhaps there was no transatlantic official recognition of the shipyard's in-house qualifications. Perhaps they simply did not care. After all, Britain was at war and it was obvious that America's involvement, one way or another, was inevitable and unavoidable. But war always justifies many things, doesn't it?

Irrespective of this contentious issue, one comes back to the very basic one: what effect did these emergency ships have on the

First and Second World Wars? The answer regarding the First World War is simple: No real effect. Few of the ships were finished and put into commission and effective use before the end of the war to be of any appreciable value. With regard to the Second World War, the simple answer is that without them the result would have been quite different. The Battle of the Atlantic was, to my mind, the most important battle of the war. It is often under-rated. It didn't have a beginning and an end and a crescendo like, say, the Battle of Britain, the Battle of Stalingrad, the Battle of Kursk, or the Battle of the Bulge. No, it just went on and on, relentlessly from the first day to the last day of the European War. Had it been lost, had the U-boat campaign been so successful that ships were being sunk at a faster rate than they could be replaced, then Britain may have fallen before December 1941 when the USA entered the war courtesy of Japan or the 1944 invasion of Europe would have been impossible because the Atlantic bridge could not be sustained. Some supplies to the USSR would have been cut off and this may have affected the outcome on the Eastern Front. At best a stalemate may have ensued with the Axis forces. At worst, Britain may have become totally isolated, especially if and when Germany developed its faster, long-range submarines and improved its V2-type missiles.

The Atlantic bridge and the ships that formed it was essential. Without it, Britain could not have sustained itself as a community let alone a community at war trying to defend itself against Nazi aggression. With the Atlantic bridge, Britain held on through those dark months of 1940 and the first half of 1941 when nothing was going right for it. Defeats were the order of the day – unless one accepts Dunkirk as a victory of sorts. The first real glimmer of hope was 22 June 1941 when Operation 'Barbarossa' – the German invasion of the USSR – began and the second, brighter glimmer – more a starburst – was 7 December 1941, when Japan declared war on the United States followed on 11 December by Germany also declaring war on the US finally bringing that country with all its industrial might, released unconditionally into the conflict. If we think of the Atlantic bridge as it existed before the end of 1941 as a narrow, two-lane road, after that it became a multi-lane highway – a freeway, albeit perilous but becoming decreasingly so after mid-

1943. However, despite the marked increase in ships available to form that bridge – the Liberty ships, the 'Forts', 'Parks' and 'Victories' and the British-built equivalents – it was not until May 1943 that the turning point in the Battle of the Atlantic came – a year-and-a-half after America's entry into the war.

So, call them dreadful-looking objects, call them ugly ducklings, call them slow, call them scows, call them good for only five years of service, call their engines archaic, call them what you will, these basic, no-frills merchant ships did the job expected of them and more. In huge convoys they crossed the Atlantic time and time again in some cases – others, less fortunate, even torpedoed on their maiden voyages – but all loaded down below what would be allowed in peacetime, they made the difference, they brought vitally needed supplies earning their keep when one voyage was, theoretically, justification and anything beyond that considered a bonus.

Talking of bonuses, one factor probably never considered – certainly not by that remarkable man, Cyril Thompson – was the fact that the basic hull and machinery could be adapted to so many different uses. In British hands this was restricted to CAM ships, to Merchant Aircraft Carriers (not strictly Thompson's design, being diesel-engined) and to adaptations of the 'Fort', 'Park', 'Victory' and Canadian versions as maintenance ships, tankers, stores issuing ships and the like.

The American Liberties knew no bounds. If I were to put on the one page the profile drawings of a Liberty ship-derived collier, hospital ship, surveillance ship or a repair ship a student of the subject just *might* just perceive the parentage by studying the hull profile. Otherwise, for most people, recognising them all as having a Liberty ship parentage would be impossible. Twenty years after the last short-term answer, this disposable one-voyage commodity was built, some were stationed in the Pacific and Atlantic Oceans, crammed with the latest radar equipment on the lookout for high-altitude Soviet bombers bearing nuclear weapons. Who could have foreseen that?

So, what was it that made this design so adaptable? I think the answer is not actually related so much to the design, to the spacing of the frames or the strength of the hull, to the Prismatic Coefficient or Block Coefficient or anything like that but more to do with availability. It wouldn't matter how many you had if the basics weren't right to begin with. So, the basics must have been right. The hull was stable – stiff in marine parlance – and not subject to problems with topweight. That is particularly evident when you look at the many long upper decks of the hospital ship that were added which must surely have had a lot of ballast added to compensate. Similarly, the tall masts with quite massive radar antennae of the YAGR surveillance/picket ships – although notes from the association of sailors who served upon them are not favourable as to the ships' motion in a big sea!

But the simpler conversions – simpler on paper anyway – to convert dry cargo holds to tankers says something about the simplicity and strength of the hull as a structure. Similarly, the more drastic – appearance-wise at least – conversion to a collier where the engine and boiler was moved aft with few problems and a very successful outcome.

In all these cases one must ask: what would have been the outcome if these conversions had not been possible and entirely fit-for-purpose ships had to be designed from scratch? I don't think one needs a crystal ball to answer that.

One must also ask: what would have been the outcome if Cyril Thompson had not been appointed to head that vital mission and that Sunderland shipyard of Joseph L Thompson & Sons Ltd. had never designed and built *Embassage* in 1935? What if it had been a flop, or simply another tramp-steamer with mediocre performance? Where would the stimulus in the design process have come from that which developed into *Dorington Court* and beyond if it had not been for that Sunderland shipyard and its chosen engine manufacturer? As I said earlier, the importance of the Merchant Shipbuilding Mission and its significance in the development of the Liberty ship cannot be over emphasised. Without it and without Cyril Thompson in particular there would have been no Liberty ship – at least as we know it.

NOTES

Introduction

1. John Terraine, *Business in Great Waters: The U-Boat Wars 1916-1945* (London: Mandarin Paperbacks, 1989), p 87.

Chapter 1: The Battle of the Atlantic, 1914–1918

1. Michael B Miller, *International Encyclopedia of the First World War: Sea Transport and Supply*, https://encyclopedia.1914-1918-online.net/article/sea_transport_and_supply
2. Terraine, *Business in Great Waters*, p 41.
3. C Ernest Fayle, *Seaborne Trade*, Vol II (London: John Murray, 1924), p 91.
4. Terraine, *Business in Great Waters*, Appendix C, p 766.
5. V E Tarrant, *The U-Boat Offensive 1914–1945* (London: Arms and Armour, 1989), p 43.
6. Charles M Sternhell and Alan M Thorndike, *Operations Evaluation Group Report No. 51, ASW In World War 2* (Washington, DC: Office of Chief of Naval Operations, 1946).
7. Terraine, *Business in Great Waters*, p 15.
8. Ibid, p 137.
9. Ibid, Appendix C, p 766.

Chapter 2: Britain's Emergency Ships of the First World War

1. W H Mitchell and L A Sawyer, *British Standard Ships of World War I* (London: The Journal of Commerce & Shipping Telegraph, Ltd., 1968), p 75.
2. Peter Elphick, *Liberty: The Ships that Won the War* (London: Chatham Publishing, 2006), p 24.
3. S C Heal, *A Great Fleet of Ships, The Canadian Forts & Parks* (Ontario: Vanwell Publishing Limited, 1999), p 27.

Chapter 3: The United States Shipping Board and the Emergency Fleet Corporation

1. The Federal Reserve Board, *Federal Reserve Bulletin*, February 1921, p 184.

Chapter 6: Britain – 1940

1. W H Mitchell and L A Sawyer, *Empire Ships of World War II* (London: The Journal of Commerce & Shipping Telegraph, Ltd., 1965), pp 3–51.

Chapter 8: Joseph L Thompson and Sons Ltd, North Sands, Sunderland

1. Elphick, *Liberty*, p 26.
2. http://www.mariners-list.com/index.php
3. Elphick, *Liberty*, p 27.
4. Ibid.
5. Ibid.
6. Ibid, p 29.
7. Ibid, Appendix 1, p 478.

Chapter 9: The Merchant Shipbuilding Commission

1. Heal, *A Great Fleet of Ships*, p 38.
2. Elphick, *Liberty*, p 35.
3. Ibid, p 32.
4. Gus Bourneuf Jr., *Workhorse of the Fleet: A History of the Liberty Ships* (Houston: American Bureau of Shipping, 1990), p 26.
5. F C Lane, *Ships for Victory: A History of Shipbuilding Under the US Maritime Commission in World War II* (Baltimore: John Hopkins Press, 1951), pp 80–1.
6. Ibid, p 83.

Chapter 10: The Importance of *Empire Liberty*

1. Mitchell and Sawyer, *Empire Ships of World War II*, p 15.

Chapter 11: The 'Oceans' and Henry J Kaiser

1. Elphick, *Liberty*, p 44.
2. Ibid, p 47.

Chapter 12: The 'Oceans' and Gibbs & Cox

1. Bourneuf, *Workhorse of the Fleet*, p 11.
2. Spencer C Tucker (ed), *World War II at Sea: An Encyclopedia*, Vol 1 (Santa Barbara: ABC-Clio, 2011), p 305.

Chapter 13: The Birth of the Liberty Ship

1. Elphick, *Liberty*, p 18.
2. Ibid.
3. Lane, *Ships for Victory*, p 73.
4. Bourneuf, *Workhorse of the Fleet*, p 48.
5. Ibid, p 51.
6. Lane, *Ships for Victory*, p 75.
7. L A Sawyer and W H Mitchell, *The Liberty Ships: The History of the 'Emergency' Type Cargo Ships Constructed in the United States During World War Two* (Newton Abbott: David & Charles (Holdings) Ltd, 1970), p 7.
8. Bourneuf, *Workhorse of the Fleet*, p 48.
9. Ibid, p 51.
10. Lane, *Ships for Victory*, p 87.
11. Ibid, p 98.

Chapter 14: The Essence of the Liberty Ship

1. Lane, *Ships for Victory*, p 457.
2. David K Brown, *Atlantic Escorts: Ships, Weapons & Tactics in World War II* (Barnsley: Seaforth

Publishing, 2007), p 146.

3. Elphick, *Liberty*, p 46.
4. Ibid, p 68.
5. Bourneuf, *Workhorse of the Fleet*, p 38.
6. Ibid, p 40.
7. Ibid, p 45.
8. Elphick, *Liberty*, pp 78 and 106.
9. Sawyer and Mitchell, *The Liberty Ships*, pp 187–8.

Chapter 15: The Forts, Parks and Victories

1. Heal, *A Great Fleet of Ships*, p 13.
2. Brian Lavery, *River-class Frigates and the Battle of the Atlantic: A technical and social history* (London: National Maritime Museum, 2006), p 33.
3. Mitchell and Sawyer, *Empire Ships of World War II*, p viii.
4. Ibid, p 8.
5. Heal, *A Great Fleet of Ships*, p 39.

Chapter 17: The CAM Ships – Catapult Merchant Ships

1. Alan Payne, Naval Historical Society Of Australia, December 1975

https://www.navyhistory.org.au/the-catapult-fighters/

Chapter 19: HMS *Girdle Ness* and Seaslug

1. R V B Blackman (ed), *Jane's Fighting Ships, 1962-63* (London: Sampson Low, Marston & Company, 1963), p 3.
2. *Jane's Fighting Ships, 1958-59* (London: Jane's Fighting Ships Publishing Co Ltd, 1959), p 248.
3. W H Mitchell and L A Sawyer, *The Oceans, The Forts and The Parks; Merchant Shipping for British Account in North America During World War II* (London: The Journal of Commerce & Shipping Telegraph, Ltd, 1966), p 42.

Chapter 20: Liberty Ship Conversions: The Second World War then the Cold War

1. Bourneuf, *Workhorse of the Fleet*, p 102.
2. Ibid, p 105.
3. Sawyer and Mitchell, *The Liberty Ships*, p 191.
4. E B Williams, *Adaptations of the Basic Liberty Design* (Society of Naval Architects and Marine Engineers, 1945), p 43.

Chapter 21: Popular Misconceptions

1. Sawyer and Mitchell, *The Liberty Ships*, p 12.
2. http://www.bbc.co.uk/ahistoryoftheworld
3. Norman Polmar and Norman B Allen, *World War II: The Encyclopedia of the War Years, 1941-1945* (New York: Dover Publications, 2012), p 503.
4. Roy Fenton, *Tramp Ships: An Illustrated History* (Barnsley: Seaforth Publishing, 2013), p 22.
5. Ibid.
6. Archibald Hurd, *The Triumph of the Tramp Ship* (London: Cassell & Company Ltd, 1922), pp 163–5.
7. Fenton, *Tramp Ships*, p 35.
8. Ibid, p 38.

Conclusion

1. Elphick, *Liberty*, p 78.
2. Ibid, p 225.
3. Ibid, p 79.
4. Lane, *Ships for Victory*, p 88

BIBLIOGRAPHY

Published Works

Blackman, R V B (ed), *Jane's Fighting Ships, 1962-63* (London: Sampson Low, Marston & Co Ltd., 1963).

Bourneuf, Gus, Jr., *Workhorse of the Fleet: A History of the Liberty Ships* (Houston: American Bureau of Shipping, 1990).

Brown, David K, *Atlantic Escorts: Ships, Weapons & Tactics in World War II* (Barnsley: Seaforth Publishing, 2007).

Chesneau, Roger, *Aircraft Carriers of the World, 1914 to the Present. An Illustrated Encyclopedia* (London: Arms and Armour Press, 1984).

Ellis, John, *The World War II Data Book: the essential facts and figures for all the combatants* (London: Aurum, 1993).

Elphick, Peter, *Liberty: The Ships that Won the War* (London: Chatham Publishing, 2006).

Fayle, C Ernest, *Seaborne Trade*, Vol II (London: John Murray, 1924).

Fenton, Roy, *Tramp Ships: An Illustrated History* (Barnsley: Seaforth Publishing, 2013).

Friedman, Norman, *British Destroyers & Frigates; The Second World War and After* (Barnsley: Seaforth Publishing, 2006).

Hague, Arnold, *The Allied Convoy System 1939-1945: Its Organization, Defence and Operation* (London: Greenhill Books, 2000).

Heal, S C, *A Great Fleet of Ships, The Canadian Forts & Parks* (Ontario: Vanwell Publishing Limited, 1999).

Hobbs, David, *British Aircraft Carriers; Design, Development and Service Histories* (Barnsley: Seaforth Publishing, 2013).

Hurd, Archibald, *The Triumph of the Tramp Ship* (Cassell & Company Limited, London, 1922).

Jane's Fighting Ships, 1958-59 (London: Jane's Fighting Ships Publishing Co Ltd, 1959).

Lavery, Brian, *River-class Frigates and the Battle of the Atlantic: A technical and social history* (London: National Maritime Museum, 2006).

Lane, F C, *Ships for Victory: A History of Shipbuilding Under the US Maritime Commission in World War II* (Baltimore: John Hopkins Press, 1951).

Marder, A J, *From the Dreadnought to Scapa Flow, Vol IV, Years of Crisis* (Barnsley: Seaforth Publishing, 2013).

Mitchell, W H, and Sawyer, L A, *British Standard Ships of World War I* (London: The Journal of Commerce & Shipping Telegraph, Ltd, 1968).

————————————, *Empire Ships of World War II* (London: The Journal of Commerce & Shipping Telegraph, Ltd., 1965).

————————————, *The Oceans, The Forts and The Parks; Merchant Shipping for British Account in North America During World War II* (London: The Journal of Commerce & Shipping Telegraph, Ltd., 1966).

Polmar, Norman, and Allen, Norman B, *World War II: The Encyclopedia of the War Years, 1941-1945* (New York: Dover Publications, 2012).

Poolman, Kenneth, *Allied Escort Carriers of World War Two in Action* (London: Blandford Press, 1988).

Sawyer, L A, and Mitchell, W H, *The Liberty Ships: The History of the 'Emergency' Type Cargo Ships Constructed in the United States During World War Two* (Newton Abbott: David & Charles (Holdings) Limited, 1970).

Sternhell, Charles M, and Thorndike, Alan M, *Operations Evaluation Group Report No. 51, ASW In World War 2* (Washington, DC: Office of Chief of Naval Operations, 1946).

Tarrant, V E, *The U-Boat Offensive 1914–1945* (London: Arms and Armour Press, 1989).

Terraine, John, *Business in Great Waters: The U-Boat Wars 1916-1945* (London: Mandarin Paperbacks, 1989).

Tucker, Spencer C (ed), *World War II at Sea: An Encyclopedia,* 2 vols (Santa Barbara: ABC-Clio, 2011).

United States Maritime Commission, *America Builds Ships: The Programme of The United States Maritime Commission* (Washington DC: United States Maritime Commission, 1940).

Official Histories

Bechtel Corporation, *Bechtel: Building a Century: 1898-1998* (Kansas City, Missouri: Andrews McMeel, 1998).

Borthwick, Alastair, *Yarrow and Company Limited, The First Hundred Years* (Glasgow: The University Press, 1965).

Unpublished Works

Fischer, Gerald J, *A Statistical Summary of Shipbuilding Under the US Maritime Commission During World War II*, Historical Reports of the War Administration United States Maritime Commission, No. 2, 1949.

McKellar Norman L, 'Steel Shipbuilding under the US Shipping Board, 1917-1921', *The Belgian Shiplover* No. 87 (May–June 1962).

Mercogliano, S R, 'The United States Merchant Shipping Offensive During the Second World War', *The Northern Mariner* (October 2001).

Payne, Alan, 'The Catapult Fighters', Naval Historical Society of Australia, *The Naval Historical Review* (December 1975).

Tassava, C J, *Launching a Thousand Ships: Entrepreneurs, War Workers, and the State in American Shipbuilding, 1940-1945*, Northwestern University, Evanston, Illinois, June 2003.

The Federal Reserve Board, *Federal Reserve Bulletin, (Final Edition)* (Washington DC: Government Printing Office, February 1921).

Williams, E B, *Adaptations of the Basic Liberty Design*, Society of Naval Architects and Marine Engineers, 1945.

Websites

https://encyclopedia.1914-18-online.net
http://www.bbc.co.uk/ahistoryoftheworld
https://www.marad.dot.gov
http://www.mariners-l.co.uk/OCEAN.html
http://www.mariners-list.com
http://www.museumradarandcommunications2006.org.uk
http://www.searlecanada.org/sunderland
http://www.shipbuildinghistory.com
http://www.shippingwondersoftheworld.com
http://www.ssarkansan.com
http://www.tynebuiltships.co.uk
http://www.theshipslist.com
https://www.wrecksite.eu

INDEX